GRIT & GRACE

TAMING TOUGH TIMES

AMARJEET SINGH TAK

Made with ❤ on the Notion Press Platform
www.notionpress.com

INVICTUS

Out of the night that covers me,
Black as the pit from pole to pole,
I thank whatever gods may be
For my unconquerable soul.

In the fell clutch of circumstance
I have not winced nor cried aloud.
Under the bludgeonings of chance
My head is bloody, but unbowed.

Beyond this place of wrath and tears
Looms but the Horror of the shade,
And yet the menace of the years
Finds and shall find me unafraid.

It matters not how strait the gate,
How charged with punishments the scroll,
I am the master of my fate,
I am the captain of my soul.

— William Ernest Henley

"Invictus" by William Ernest Henley conveys a powerful message about resilience and determination in the face of adversity. It inspires individuals to take control of their own destinies and remain unbroken by life's challenges, no matter how daunting they may seem.

Contents

Acknowledgements *vii*

Preface *ix*

Prologue *xi*

1. "Suffering And Sacrifice" 1

2. "Bouncing Back Stronger" 7

3. "Embracing Change" 12

4. "Falling Forward" 20

5. "The Odyssey Of Mindset Mastery" 25

6. "Science Of Stress Bursting" 37

7. "Building Strong Relationships" 44

8. "Goal Setting" 54

9. "Adversity As Opportunity" 61

10. "Self-compassion & Self-Care" 69

Strategies for Taming The Tough Times" 77

Acknowledgements

Dear Friends, Family, and Colleagues,

I wanted to take a moment to express my deepest gratitude and appreciation to each and every one of you for your unwavering support and love on this incredible journey with my book, "Grit & Grace." Your presence in my life has been nothing short of remarkable, and your encouragement has fueled my passion and determination.

First and foremost, I must acknowledge my rock, my love, and my life partner, Gurpreet Kour. Your belief in me has been a guiding light, shining even brighter than my own self-doubts. You inspire me to be gritty when times are tough, and your unwavering support has been the bedrock upon which I built this book. You are my pillar of strength, and I am eternally grateful for your presence in my life.

To my growing son, Ranvijay, and my darling daughter, Gracelyn, your zest for life and infectious smiles infuses my days with grace and joy. You are the driving force behind the essence of this book, reminding me every day of the beauty in resilience and the boundless love that surrounds us.

My heartfelt appreciation goes out to my father, Chandan Singh Tak, whose life has been an embodiment of resilience. Your example has been a constant source of inspiration, teaching me that with determination and grit, we can overcome any obstacle. And to my beloved mother, Sharda Devi, your unconditional love has been my refuge. Your unwavering belief in me has been the foundation upon which I've built my dreams, and I feel blessed to have you in my corner.

To all my friends, family, and colleagues, your support has been the wind beneath my wings. Your encouragement, feedback, and faith in my abilities have propelled me to reach for greater heights.

As I reflect on this journey, I am filled with overwhelming gratitude and a profound sense of love. "Grit & Grace" would not have been possible without each of you. Thank you for being my support system, my inspiration, and my reason for believing in the power of resilience and grace.

With heartfelt thanks and warmest regards,
Amarjeet Singh Tak

PREFACE

In the grand symphony of life, we are often met with moments that test the very notes of our existence. These moments, like unrelenting storms, can shake us to our core, leaving us bewildered and seeking harmony in the cacophony. It is in these times of adversity that we discover the true essence of our character, the grit that resides deep within us, and the grace that enables us to rise above the challenges that life presents.

Welcome to "Grit & Grace: Taming the Tough Time," a journey through the crucible of life's trials and tribulations, written by someone who has walked through the fiery furnace and emerged not only unscathed but stronger, wiser, and more resilient. I am Amarjeet Singh Tak, a Business Strategist, People Coach, and Hustler, and I am honoured to be your guide on this transformative expedition. Throughout my career, I have worn many hats, from shaping high-performing teams to navigating the labyrinthine corridors of complex markets. My passion for fostering innovation and empowering individuals has been the compass that has guided me through both the calm waters and tumultuous storms of life. With this book, I aim to share the lessons I've learned, the wisdom I've gained, and the strategies I've developed for not only surviving adversity but thriving in its midst.

"Grit & Grace" is not just a book; it's a lifeline for those facing challenging times. In its pages, you will find stories of resilience and triumph, strategies for overcoming obstacles, and a roadmap for harnessing your inner strength. This book is a testament to the enduring human spirit and the boundless potential that resides within each of us.

In the chapters that follow, you will embark on a journey of self-discovery, learning how to tap into your inner reservoir of grit—the unyielding determination that propels you forward even when the path is treacherous. You will also uncover the power of grace—the ability to find beauty, compassion, and strength in the face of adversity. We will delve into the art of strategic thinking, exploring how to navigate complex challenges with clarity and purpose. You will discover the transformative impact of innovation and learn how to adapt and thrive in an ever-changing landscape. Moreover, we will explore the profound influence of leadership, both in your personal life and in the broader world.

As you turn the pages of this book, I encourage you to reflect on your journey and the challenges you've faced. Consider this a conversation between friends, where you are not alone in your struggles. Together, we will explore the rich symphony of human experience and unearth the resilience that resides within you. I want to express my deepest gratitude for joining me on this voyage. Your presence here is a testament to your commitment to growth and your desire to transform challenges into opportunities. My hope is that "Grit & Grace" becomes a trusted companion on your journey, providing inspiration, guidance, and a sense of community as you navigate the tough times in life.

May this book serve as a beacon of hope and a source of strength, reminding you that you are powerful beyond measure. It is my privilege to share these words with you, and I look forward to walking this path together, armed with the indomitable spirit of grit and the enduring grace that resides within us all.

Prologue

Grit & Grace

"Taming Tough Times"

Dear Remarkable Souls,

It's been a whirlwind of three years since I last inked my thoughts onto paper, and I'm back with a dose of motivation, a sprinkle of insight, and a dash of that spark you need to wield your pen once more. Picture this as your friendly nudge, your resounding reason, and the secret ingredient to harnessing your innate human potential.

Remember the last time I poured my thoughts onto these pages? Ah, yes, it was during the cosmic chaos of the Covid era. In the middle of the first wave's stormy embrace, I found myself on a sabbatical, a brief reprieve from the clutches of routine. Armed with solitude and an urge to transcend the present moment, I birthed my debut book – "You Are Powerful Beyond Measure." A title etched in the fabric of unpredictability, where the world waltzed with a pandemic and uncertainty was the only certainty.

In those uncertain times, I found solace in my words. My health was a beacon of luck amidst the pandemic's shadow, but my professional world, oh, it teetered on the precipice. Penning my thoughts became my refuge, a medicinal elixir when human connection seemed distant, and conversations with confidantes were confined to the whispers of my heart. I found my escape in those pages, a canvas for my soul's yearning. And let me tell you, I unearthed a pearl of wisdom amidst the trials: Adversity is the battleground, and resilience, my dear comrades, is the sword. To steer clear of adversity's clutches, I learned to channel my energy into creation, into positivity. A lesson engraved in the scrolls of existence itself.

Fast forward to today, when the pandemic's curtain has lifted, revealing a world reshaped and reborn. Geopolitical landscapes have morphed, businesses have adapted, interactions have transmuted, and digital realms have embraced their prowess like never before. Much like the phoenix, our civilization is proving its prowess in reforming, performing, and transforming – echoing the wisdom of our revered Prime Minister, Narendra Modi.

Yet, I pondered – what's next? What topic deserves the spotlight of my second creation? Doubt whispered in my ear, taunting my credentials. I am no researcher, no celebrity, merely a business manager entwined in the threads of targets, KPIs, and SOPs. Yet, dear reader, I am a lifelong learner. My canvas extends from my journey, my observations, my tribulations – can my words ignite a spark, kindle a flame of understanding? But wait, who is my audience? A student seeking direction, a corporate warrior yearning for balance, a civil servant navigating complexities, a homemaker weaving life's tapestry, or perhaps, a budding management prodigy? Lessons of life, after all, transcend the boundaries between personal and professional domains. My insights, my triumphs, my stumbles – could they be the guiding stars for another soul's voyage?

And there it was, the question that had lingered like a faithful shadow – my second book's topic. The answer shimmered in the realm of resilience, a beacon guiding us through adversity's labyrinth. "Unlocking Your Resilience

Blueprint: Thriving in the Face of Adversity" – a testament to the unwavering spirit that fuels our journey.

Adversity, my friends, is no stranger. A whirlwind of self-doubt, physical setbacks, rejections, poverty's sting, the agony of loss, and the climb towards career pinnacles. These tempests dance through the chapters of our lives, scripting tales of struggle, transformation, and triumph. But let me enthral you with a tale from the annals of time, Once upon a time, in a land where wisdom and enlightenment blossomed like the sweetest of flowers, there lived a woman named Kisa Gotami. Her story is one of profound sorrow and transformation, a tale that carries a timeless lesson for all, especially the young and curious hearts.

Kisa Gotami's journey began when she married at a tender age and was blessed with a son, her pride and joy. Her world was illuminated by the radiant smile of her child, and every day seemed to overflow with happiness. But as the fickle hands of fate would have it, one day, a shadow crept over her life.

Her beloved son fell terribly ill, his laughter silenced by the relentless grip of sickness. Kisa Gotami, a mother's love burning fiercely within her, did everything she could to save him. She sought the help of healers, chanted prayers, and cradled him through endless nights, but fate, in its unyielding decree, chose to take her son away.

Devastated, Kisa Gotami refused to accept the brutal truth – that her son was no longer among the living. Clutching her lifeless child to her chest, she wandered through her village, her tearful eyes pleading with every neighbor and passerby, "Can anyone bring my son back to life?"

The villagers, their hearts heavy with sympathy, saw the reality that Kisa Gotami couldn't grasp. Her son was gone, and no magic in this world could turn back time. They gently advised her to accept her son's fate and prepare for his final journey. But Kisa Gotami, lost in her grief, could not let go. She sank to her knees, her voice trembling as she whispered to her son's still form, "Wake up, my child, wake up."

In the midst of her despair, a wise elder of the village took pity on her. He spoke gently, "Kisa Gotami, we cannot help you. But there is one who might. Go to the Buddha. Perhaps he can bring your son back to life." With newfound hope, Kisa Gotami hurried to the Buddha's residence and fell at his feet, her tears flowing like a river. "Please, Great Buddha," she implored, "bring my son back to life." The Buddha, his eyes filled with compassion, looked upon her and said, "Kisa Gotami, I have a way to bring your son back to life." Kisa Gotami's heart soared with hope. "My Lord, I will do anything, anything to bring my son back to me." The Buddha spoke gently, "If that is your wish, then go and find me a mustard seed. But there's a condition, Kisa Gotami. The mustard seed must come from a house where no one residing there has ever lost a family member to death. Bring me this seed, and your son will come back to life."

Kisa Gotami embarked on her quest, moving from house to house, asking for a mustard seed. At the first house, a young woman offered her some mustard seeds. But when Kisa Gotami inquired if they had ever lost a family member to death, the young woman confessed that her grandmother had passed away just a few months ago.

She moved on to the second house, where her husband had died a few years earlier. The third house had lost an uncle, and the fourth, an aunt. And so it went on, house after house, with the same painful refrain – every home had experienced the sting of death.

As she journeyed, Kisa Gotami's heart grew heavy with realization. She understood that death was an inevitable part of life, a universal truth that touched every soul. With this profound insight, she put aside her grief, for she knew her son could not return.

In the depths of the forest, she buried her beloved child, letting him rest in peace among the trees and the whispers of nature. Kisa Gotami, now transformed by her journey, returned to the Buddha, and became one of his most devoted followers, sharing the wisdom she had gained with all who sought solace and enlightenment. The moral of Kisa Gotami's tale is as timeless as her story itself – that death, like life, is an integral part of our existence. It is a lesson that reminds us to cherish each moment, to embrace the impermanence of life, and to find the strength to let go when the time comes. Through Kisa Gotami's journey, we learn that in the face of grief and loss, there is the potential for growth, understanding, and profound transformation, ultimately leading us on a path toward enlightenment and inner peace.

No soul treads the earthly path unscathed by adversity's touch – suffering, loss, rejection, pain, they are our steadfast companions. And as the adage goes, no pain, no gain. Yet, within the tapestry of tribulation lies the seed of realization, the bloom of acceptance. In facing life's crucible, we question, we stumble, we rise. Each challenge is a stepping stone, each hardship a rung on the ladder of evolution. Just as in the halls of academia, we traverse exams to prove our knowledge, life too is an eternal classroom. Adversity serves as the syllabus, resilience as our guide, and growth as the coveted diploma. Our journey is an ever-evolving saga, where suffering is but a prelude to ascension.

Dear reader, as you dive into the pages that follow, envision resilience as your compass, adversity as your mentor, and transformation as your muse. The path you tread, the choices you make, the resilience you nurture – they shape the narrative of your life. The tale you craft, whether protagonist or antagonist, is an ode to your fortitude, your triumph over tribulation.

So, buckle up, adventurers of the spirit, and prepare to unlock your personal Resilience Blueprint. Let these pages be your roadmap, your companion, and your inspiration. For within them lies the alchemy of thriving in the face of adversity – a journey that promises to unveil the hero within.

With unwavering anticipation,
Altruist Amarjeet

I

"Suffering and Sacrifice"

The Unseen Price of Greatness

In the journey towards success and the pursuit of achieving extraordinary things, there's a powerful truth we can't ignore: pain and suffering are often woven into the very fabric of these remarkable adventures. The road to triumph is usually built through the fires of hardship, unrelenting determination, and sheer struggle. If we look back at history, we'll see this pattern repeated in the life stories of various people, including entrepreneurs, politicians, athletes, saints, and even legendary figures.

Let's take a closer look at the ancient story of Lord Rama, a tale that still resonates with us today. This brave and noble king, who was adorned with the splendor of a grand coronation, suddenly found himself plunged into the depths of suffering. Alongside his beloved wife Sita and his faithful brother, he embarked on a fourteen-year exile – a journey that forced them into the harsh, unforgiving wilderness, far from the comforts of their kingdom. They roamed like wanderers, facing one challenge after another. Yet, amidst these trials, Rama's unwavering love for Sita drove him to confront the most powerful ruler of his time, the mysterious king of Lanka. He engaged in a battle that seemed impossible to win, an epic showdown filled with love and sacrifice. Rama's journey teaches us the profound truth that greatness often emerges from enduring pain.

In this grand mosaic of greatness, another radiant figure comes into focus: Lord Krishna. He was born into a world filled with tragedy, losing six siblings before he even took his first breath. Danger clung to his early days, leading to his separation from his parents. His childhood was marked by numerous attempts on his life, a testament to his unbreakable spirit. And then came the heart-wrenching moment when he had to leave his beloved home in Vrindavan and the love of his life, Radha. All of this was done to reclaim his kingdom and free his birth parents. The story of Krishna serves as a reminder of the immense sacrifices one must make on the path to true greatness.

In the end, these stories show us that the pursuit of greatness often involves enduring tremendous pain and overcoming seemingly insurmountable challenges. It's through these trials that individuals like Rama and Krishna have left an indelible mark on history, reminding us that greatness is worth the price one pays for it. Take a moment to think about a man named Jesus, a shining example of unwavering values. His life story leads us to a moment of intense suffering that has echoed through the ages: the crucifixion. It was a form of torture that's hard to imagine in its sheer brutality. Nails weren't driven through the palms as you might have seen in pictures; they were hammered through His wrists, tearing tendons and forcing Him to rely on back muscles just to breathe. His feet were nailed together, making Him switch between arching His back and using His legs to gasp for air. His suffering captured the very essence of pain, all because He stood by His principles. This is the incredible price of true greatness.

Now, let's turn our attention to Guru Gobind Singh Sahib, revered as Sarbans Dani, the Merciful Donor who gave everything. He left an unforgettable mark on humanity, not by seeking power or land, but by fighting for justice and righteousness in the name of Sikhism. The heart-wrenching sacrifice of his young sons, Fateh Singh, and Zorawar Singh, stands as a powerful symbol of their unwavering beliefs. They were tortured and bricked alive in Punjab, and their sacrifice still resonates today. Even Guru Sahib's elder sons, who became martyrs in the battle of Chamkaur alongside 40 brave Sikhs, defied unimaginable odds by taking on an army of over 10 lakh. Their courage and faith in the face of suffering remind us of the incredible heights humanity can reach, even in the darkest moments.

These stories of sacrifice and suffering in the grand symphony of history stir our deepest emotions. They show us that the path to greatness is often filled with challenges that test our limits. In the crucible of pain, there's a transformative power that propels us toward our destinies.

As author Jodi Picoult wisely said, "The human capacity for burden is like bamboo—far more flexible than you'd ever believe at first glance." In the intricate tapestry of life, success often hides behind a curtain of trials and tribulations. While we may admire the achievements of famous and successful individuals, it's important to remember that their journeys were often marked by hardships and sacrifices that shaped their destinies. Let's now explore the lives of three modern icons – one from business, one from sports, and one from politics or social service – who turned their suffering into stepping stones towards greatness.

In the world of business, there's a lot more than meets the eye. It's a place where people face tough times and have to dig deep to overcome obstacles. One person who truly exemplifies this spirit of innovation and daring is Elon Musk. You might have heard of him as the guy behind electric cars, space exploration, and clean energy. But his journey was far from smooth.

Elon Musk grew up in South Africa, and from an early age, he was a curious thinker who dreamed big. However, life threw some hard punches at him. In his early days, he had money troubles and even had to sleep in his office. His first business venture, Zip2, which aimed to create business directories and maps for newspapers, faced countless challenges. It was on the brink of failure, but Elon's determination saved the day. He managed to secure important partnerships, and eventually, Compaq bought Zip2 for a staggering $300 million.

But Elon's ambitions didn't stop there. He co-founded X.com, which later became PayPal, changing the way we make payments online. Yet, even this journey had its share of setbacks. Elon was actually kicked out of his own company after a merger, a tough blow. Instead of giving up, he turned that pain into determination. With the money he got from selling PayPal, Elon went on to create SpaceX, Tesla, and SolarCity – three companies that would reshape space travel, cars, and clean energy solutions.

In the world of sports, there's another incredible story – that of Mary Kom. She comes from Manipur in the northeastern part of India, and her journey to becoming a world-famous boxer was full of unique challenges.

Mary loved boxing, but in her society, it wasn't common for women to enter male-dominated sports. Still, she didn't let that stop her. She faced societal norms along with her opponents in the boxing ring. Money was tight, and she had limited resources and no proper training facilities. But each obstacle only fueled her determination to excel. Perhaps her most challenging moment came during her pregnancy when many believed her boxing career was over. But Mary Kom, true to her fighting spirit, proved them wrong. She became a mother and then made a triumphant comeback. Her shining moment came when she won an Olympic bronze medal in 2012. It not only made India proud but also showed the world the power of determination and sacrifice.

Now, in the realm of social service, there's Kailash Satyarthi, a true champion for the marginalized and oppressed. His relentless mission was to protect children's rights and put an end to child labor, and it left a significant mark on society. Kailash's work was dangerous. He would actively raid factories and workshops to rescue children from terrible working conditions. Despite threats to his life and powerful interests working against him, he didn't give in. His organization, Bachpan Bachao Mandolin (Save the Childhood Movement), became a platform for change and justice. Kailash's sacrifices were evident when he received the Nobel Peace Prize in 2014 for his unwavering dedication to children's rights. His life's work transformed countless lives and showed that one person's determination can ignite a movement that changes society for the better.

In the end, these three remarkable individuals remind us that greatness often emerges from the toughest of times. Suffering and sacrifices can be like a furnace that forges our resilience and determination. They show us that challenges are not roadblocks but stepping stones on our path to excellence.

As we face our own challenges, let's draw inspiration from these modern icons. When life gets tough, remember that we have a choice – we can either give up or rise above. The road to success may be paved with sacrifices, but it's these very sacrifices that push us towards our dreams. Just like a phoenix rising from the ashes, individuals who use their suffering as a catalyst for triumph can achieve incredible things.

In the end, the value of suffering and sacrifice lies not only in the achievements they bring but, in the transformation, they create within us. They teach us that setbacks are not defeats but opportunities to rewrite the stories of our lives. So, as we face our own challenges, let's embrace the example set by these modern icons, and may our struggles become the foundation of our own stories of triumph.

> "*Pain is the price you pay for resting life - Anonymous*"

II

"Bouncing Back Stronger"

The Power of Resilience

In the vibrant city of Mumbai, where people chase their dreams like the waves crash against the Marine Drive, amazing stories of resilience have unfolded. These stories, from all over the world, reveal the incredible power of bouncing back when life throws you a curveball, a trait that makes some people truly extraordinary.

Resilience isn't just a fancy word; it's a quality that separates the everyday folks from the extraordinary ones. It's the superpower to survive the toughest times and come out even stronger. But what exactly is resilience, and how do some people and companies become masters at bouncing back from challenges? Let's take a journey to uncover the secrets of resilience, understanding the science and the emotions that make it happen.

Imagine you're walking through the busy streets of New York City, where the skyscrapers reach for the clouds and dreams seem boundless. Now, picture a young woman named Sara Blakely. She had an idea that was out of the ordinary - to create comfy, practical undergarments that wouldn't show under clothing. But her journey to success was filled with rejections. People said her idea was crazy and that the world didn't need what she had to offer. But Sara never gave up. With her unstoppable spirit, she kept knocking on doors until one 'yes' changed her life forever. Sara Blakely's story of creating Spanx teaches us an incredible lesson about resilience. She believed in her vision when no one else did, and she was ready to face rejection after rejection until she achieved her dream. It's that inner voice that says, "I won't give up" When things get tough that often makes all the difference. Now, let's hop over to the heart of Silicon Valley, where innovation is the name of the game. Here, we meet a company that redefined resilience - Apple Inc. The company's co-founder, Steve Jobs, faced countless setbacks in his career, including getting kicked out of the very company he helped build. Yet, Steve's unbreakable determination and creativity allowed him to stage one of the most amazing comebacks in business history. Steve's ability to embrace failure and turn it into a learning experience shows us another side of resilience. It's about seeing failure as a way to grow, not as a defeat. Apple's revival wasn't just about new products; it was a sign of their ability to adapt, evolve, and learn from their mistakes.

Resilience isn't only about the mind; it's connected to our bodies too. In the heart of Hollywood, the story of Dwayne "The Rock" Johnson unfolds. Before becoming a famous actor, Johnson had his heart set on a football career.

But his dreams crumbled when he was cut from the Canadian Football League, leaving him with only seven dollars in his pocket. But Johnson's journey took an unexpected turn. He embraced his passion for wrestling and, through sheer determination, transformed into a global icon.

Dwayne Johnson's story shines a light on the physical side of resilience. Our bodies are built to handle stress, both mentally and physically. Hormones like cortisol surge during tough times, giving us the energy to tackle challenges head-on. When managed effectively, this surge can push individuals to rise above adversity, just like The Rock did. Johnson's resilience wasn't just in his mind; it was also in his body's ability to adapt and respond.

So, the next time life throws you a curveball, remember these incredible stories of resilience. It's not just about being mentally tough, but also about believing in yourself, learning from failure, and knowing that your body is designed to help you bounce back stronger than ever. You've got what it takes to be extraordinary, just like Sara Blakely, Steve Jobs, and Dwayne Johnson.

As we travel back to India, we meet someone who embodies the never-give-up spirit - Ratan Tata. In the world of business, he's like a superhero who led the Tata Group through some tough times. One shining example of his resilience was the launch of the Tata Nano. At first, everyone was excited, but then, unexpected problems popped up, like protests land acquisition and having to move factories. But Ratan Tata didn't back down. He showed us that resilience isn't just about success; it's also about having the guts to face failures and setbacks.

Ratan Tata's story tells us that resilience isn't just for people; it's for companies too. Whether a company sinks or swims during tough times depends on its leaders' determination to keep going. It's like how a tree's roots dig deeper during a storm - a company's values and leadership get tested and become stronger during challenges. So, what's our big takeaway from these stories of resilience? It's not just a fancy word; it's like a superpower that helps people, companies, and even whole countries keep moving forward. It's about believing in yourself, learning from your mistakes, rolling with the punches, and facing tough times with bravery.

Now, let's jet off to Japan, where they turned their resilience into a national success story after the destruction of World War II. Picture this: It's 1945, and Japan is in ruins after World War II. Everything's a mess - cities are piles of rubble, roads are gone, and the economy is a disaster. But in the midst of all this despair, a spark of resilience started to shine through. Japanese people, who've always believed in never giving up and helping each other out, decided to rebuild their country.

This Japanese resilience wasn't just random; it was rooted in their history and culture. They have a word, "*gaman,*" which means enduring tough stuff with patience and dignity. This cultural spirit of resilience became their guiding light in the darkest days. The Japanese folks joined forces, united by a common goal - rebuilding their nation.

In the years that followed, Japan's recovery was nothing short of incredible. With hard work, adaptability, and a drive to move forward, they rebuilt cities, fixed their economy, and became a global powerhouse. The same qualities that fueled their resilience during hard times turned Japan into a world leader. The story of Japan teaches us that a nation's resilience isn't just luck; it's a mix of their culture, history, and the determination of their people.

Japan's rise from the ashes isn't just about getting back what was lost; it's about using the lessons learned from tough times to build a better future.

In today's world, when countries face all sorts of challenges - like economic slumps, natural disasters, or political chaos - Japan's story reminds us that resilience has the power to shape a nation's destiny. It's proof that no matter how tough things get, with determination, unity, and an unbreakable spirit, you can overcome setbacks.

As we think about the stories of people and nations with incredible resilience, remember that it's not just a trait; it's a force that pushes individuals and nations forward. Whether it's Sara Blakely who refused to give up, Apple who learned from failure, Dwayne Johnson whose body helped him rise, or Japan that rebuilt from the rubble, they all share the ability to bounce back, even stronger.

> “*"Fall seven times, stand up eight." - Japanese Proverb*”

So, when you face your own challenges and setbacks, take inspiration from these stories. Let the spirit of resilience be your guide, knowing that just like individuals and nations have triumphed over adversity, you too can navigate life's storms and come out stronger. The journey might be tough, but remember, it's in the face of challenges that the most remarkable stories of resilience are written.

III

"Embracing Change"

Navigating Uncertainty

In the grand tapestry of life, change is the golden thread that stitches together every chapter. Since time immemorial, the world has evolved, civilizations have flourished and crumbled, and individuals have ridden the tides of shifting circumstances. In today's ever-shifting landscape, change isn't merely a constant; it's a potent accelerant. The skill of embracing change, adapting, and thriving in the face of uncertainty has become the hallmark of success. As we embark on this journey of exploration, we will delve deep into the art of embracing change, drawing inspiration from the realms of sports, business, technology, and celebrity stories. At the heart of it all, we'll discover the essence of "Grit and grace."

Embracing Change—An Opportunity for Growth

In the realm of cricket, where legends are etched into history's scrolls, there stands a figure who embodies solidity, patience, and unyielding perseverance. Rahul Dravid, affectionately known as "The Wall," was more than a cricketer; he was a living testament to the power of adaptability and evolution in the ever-shifting world of sports. In the hallowed halls of cricketing history, Dravid's initial success with the Indian cricket team shines like a radiant star. His cricketing prowess wielded magic as he defied bowlers with a technique that seemed impervious. The numbers speak volumes about his brilliance – over 13,000 Test runs and 10,000 One Day International (ODI) runs. His ability to stand resolute while wickets tumbled around him earned him the revered title of "The Wall." Yet, like every compelling narrative, change came knocking at the door.

The cricketing world was in flux, the pace was quickening, and age-old norms were evolving. The era of mammoth sixes and swift runs was dawning, and the patient, technique-driven approach was perceived as a relic of the past. In the midst of this transformation, Dravid faced a pivotal juncture. The very qualities that had once made him a stalwart were now regarded as limitations. His scoring rate was deemed sluggish, and he found himself omitted from the team.

Amidst the whirlwind of change, Dravid could have quietly faded into the backdrop, becoming a footnote in cricket's annals. However, he opted for a different path, one that showcased his extraordinary ability to adapt without sacrificing his principles. He acknowledged that the game's rules were shifting, but he also recognized that his identity as a batsman was deeply rooted in his technique. Dravid understood that change didn't necessitate a complete overhaul of one's identity.

With the same indomitable spirit that characterized his time at the crease, Dravid returned, donning the gloves of a wicketkeeper. He embraced a new role, adding a fresh dimension to his game. This shift in approach wasn't just about securing his place; it was about thriving amidst change. And thrive he did. In the modern era of ODIs, Dravid showcased his versatility, accumulating runs at a pace that confounded his critics. The wall wasn't crumbling; it was adapting, evolving, and standing tall in the face of transformation.

However, the cricketing cosmos held more surprises. As T20 cricket stormed onto the scene, with its power-packed performances and lightning-fast matches, Dravid didn't shy away from the challenge. Instead of surrendering his technique to fleeting trends, he embraced the essence of T20 cricket without forsaking his core strengths. The evolution continued, and Dravid emerged as one of the most sought-after players in this dynamic format. But Dravid's tale doesn't conclude with his playing days. His journey of adaptability found new chapters as he captained India in ODIs and led the Rajasthan Royals in the Indian Premier League (IPL). His leadership mirrored his approach as a player—firmly rooted in tradition yet open to innovation.

In a world that often celebrates the flashy and transient, Rahul Dravid's odyssey stands as a testament to the power of embracing change while remaining true to oneself. His story reminds us that evolution need not erase identity; it can magnify it. Dravid's transformation from "The Wall" to a versatile player and leader serves as an invaluable lesson for all generations.

As we tread the path of our own lives, we are destined to encounter change. Dravid's journey reminds us that change isn't an adversary; it's an ally that challenges us to elevate our game. Like a seasoned cricketer who adjusts his stance to face a new delivery, we too must adapt, adapt, and improvise. In the ever-evolving game of life, embracing change isn't just a skill; it's a masterpiece waiting to be painted with our own unique blend of "Grit and grace."

Strategies for Adapting to New Circumstances

In the bustling world of business, where giants rise and fall like skyscrapers against the economic horizon, one company not only stood resilient but also radiated in the face of adversity. Reliance Industries, India's corporate behemoth, confronted the tempestuous waves of the COVID-19 pandemic head-on, wielding its digital acumen as a formidable shield and emerging not only unscathed but stronger than ever before.

Before the world fell into the clutches of the pandemic, Reliance Industries was already a formidable force, boasting an impressive array of businesses spanning petrochemicals, refining, retail, and telecommunications. It had built an empire over decades, a legacy of success that many envied. Then, COVID-19 struck, plunging markets into chaos and casting an ominous shadow of uncertainty over even the mightiest of corporations.

However, as every great story would have it, this is where the plot thickens. Reliance Industries was not about to be outdone by a mere virus. Armed with its digital artillery and an audacious spirit, the conglomerate executed a pivot that left many in awe. The blueprint was simple: embrace the digital wave sweeping across industries, for even in the midst of chaos, opportunities abound.

As the world retreated into the safety of their homes, digital connectivity became the lifeline that held society together. Reliance Industries, with its telecom arm Jio, had already laid the foundation for this digital revolution. Riding this wave, they navigated the storm by offering affordable data plans, seamlessly enabling work-from-home, online learning, and digital entertainment. In the time it took to binge-watch a series, Jio became India's lifeline, ensuring that the virtual world was just as alive as the physical.

Yet, Reliance's digital evolution wasn't confined to home screens; it transcended borders, forging alliances that left the world stunned. In a strategic move that turned heads, Reliance partnered with tech titans Facebook, Google, and Microsoft. These weren't mere collaborations; they were tectonic shifts that signaled Reliance Industries' determination to rewrite the rules of the game. These alliances were more than business ventures; they were about reshaping the digital landscape, a declaration that Reliance Industries was here to dominate the tech-savvy era.

In the turbulent sea of stock markets, Reliance Industries faced a storm of its own. Share values plummeted, and pessimists whispered their doubts. However, Reliance's tale is not one of capitulation; it's a saga of resurgence. With each strategic move and every innovation, they not only weathered the storm but rose like a phoenix from the ashes. Their digital investments paid off, their alliances bore fruit, and their commitment to innovation set them on a path that defied even the harshest of forecasts.

And so, with the dust settling and the world gingerly resuming its pace, Reliance Industries emerged victorious.

It transformed crisis into opportunity and uncertainty into audacity. The numbers tell a story of their own: Before the pandemic, their market capitalization was impressive. Post-crisis, their market cap soared to even greater heights. With renewed vigor, they became the most valuable company in India, and their success resonated across industries.

Reliance Industries' journey isn't just a narrative; it's a masterclass in adaptability, innovation, and tenacity. From riding the digital wave to rewriting the rules through strategic alliances, they have demonstrated that even in the toughest of times, victory isn't merely possible; it's inevitable for those who dare to embrace change.

As we stand on the precipice of our own challenges, we look to Reliance Industries as a beacon of inspiration. Their story isn't solely about business; it's about the indomitable spirit that refuses to yield in the face of adversity. It's about leveraging our strengths, forging alliances, and weaving opportunity from uncertainty. Reliance Industries' journey is a reminder that the world may change, but the power of humans will remain a constant force, steering us towards success, even when the odds are stacked against us.

> “*"The secret of change is to focus all of your energy, not on fighting the old, but on building the new."*
> *— Socrates*”

Wisdom from the Ages—A Biblical Perspective on Change

In the grand symphony of human wisdom, biblical scriptures offer profound insights into change. Ecclesiastes 3:1 reminds us that "To everything, there is a season and a time to every purpose under the heaven." This ancient wisdom reverberates across time, teaching us that change is a fundamental aspect of existence. To resist it is to deny the very essence of life's rhythm.

> "*"For I know the plans I have for you, declares the Lord, plans for welfare and not for evil, to give you a future and a hope."*
> *— Jeremiah 29:11*"

As we traverse the landscapes of sports, business, technology, and the lives of celebrities, we are reminded that embracing change is not a passive act—it's a dynamic dance with life's unfolding story. Change is the chisel that sculpts our character, the forge that tempers our mettle, and the canvas on which we paint the masterpiece of our lives.

Embrace Change, Craft Your Destiny

In this journey of exploration, we have uncovered the stories of individuals and entities that have embraced change with open arms. From Rahul Dravid's mastery of adaptation to Reliance Industries' lesson in adapting to the march of technology, each story echoes the same truth: change is an opportunity, not an obstacle.

In the grand symphony of existence, change is the melody that weaves through every note. It's a reminder that in the face of uncertainty, we hold the power to choose our response. We can choose to resist, to falter, or we can choose to embrace, adapt, and soar to new heights. The stories we've explored are not just anecdotes; they are invitations to embrace the change that shapes our destiny. So, as you stand at the crossroads of change, remember that the canvas of your life awaits your brushstrokes. Embrace change as a partner in your journey, a collaborator in your growth, and a catalyst for your transformation. For in the embrace of change lies the power to craft your destiny, to paint your story with hues of resilience, innovation, and unyielding spirit. Embrace change with "Grit and grace," and watch as your life becomes a masterpiece that leaves the world in awe.

IV

"Falling Forward"

ISRO's Lessons in Embracing Failure

In the quiet, starlit night of September 6, 2019, something extraordinary was about to happen. The world held its breath as the Indian Space Research Organization (ISRO) attempted a historic soft landing on the uncharted territory of the moon's south pole. The mission was Chandrayaan-2, a testament to human ingenuity, ambition, and the unyielding spirit of exploration. It was a mission defined by two words: Grit and grace. Chandrayaan-2 aimed to land an unmanned rover on the moon's south pole for research and exploration. The world watched with bated breath as ISRO set its sights on this lunar milestone. The excitement was palpable, and expectations were high. The global space community stood in awe of what India was about to achieve. As the spacecraft began its descent, the control room at ISRO's headquarters in Bengaluru was filled with tension and anticipation. Success seemed within grasp. The engineers and scientists, men, and women of

ISRO, embodied the essence of Grit and grace, as they watched their years of hard work and dedication unfold before their eyes.

However, the universe had other plans that night. At an altitude of just 2.1 kilometers from the lunar surface, something went awry. The Vikram lander, tasked with carrying the Pragyan rover, lost communication with mission control, leaving the world in suspense. Seconds turned into minutes, minutes into hours, and eventually, ISRO had to accept the harsh reality - the mission had not gone as planned. Chandrayaan-2 had faltered. The failure was a gut-wrenching moment for ISRO and the entire nation. But what came next was even more remarkable. In the face of adversity, ISRO displayed an unwavering commitment to its mission, values, and the pursuit of knowledge. They displayed Grit and grace, not by avoiding failure, but by embracing it.

The first lesson we can draw from this chapter of ISRO's journey is the acceptance of failure. In our personal and professional lives, we often encounter setbacks and disappointments. It's easy to feel defeated, but the key is to approach failure with the same resilience and poise that ISRO did. Failure is not a dead end; it's a stepping stone on the path to success. ISRO's response to the Chandrayaan-2 setback was both humbling and inspiring. Instead of dwelling on the past, they turned their attention to the future. They began an exhaustive analysis of what had gone wrong and what could be done to ensure success in the next mission. This marked the start of a transformative journey.

One of the first lessons ISRO learned from the Chandrayaan-2 failure was the need for a robust and redundant system. To become failure-proof, they decided to implement standby mechanisms for critical components of the mission. This was a clear example of how Grit and grace led them to be prepared for unforeseen challenges. In our own lives, we can apply this lesson by building redundancy into our plans and projects. Having a backup plan or alternative strategies can make a world of difference when we encounter unexpected obstacles. It's a testament to our resilience and adaptability.

The redesign of the lander and rover was a monumental task. ISRO's scientists and engineers worked tirelessly to improve the mission's design. They refined the navigation systems, ensuring pinpoint accuracy for landing on the moon's treacherous surface. This attention to detail demonstrated the significance of continuous improvement, another valuable lesson for young professionals. In our careers, we should always strive to enhance our skills, knowledge, and methodologies. Just like ISRO, we must be willing to revisit our designs and strategies, seeking opportunities for refinement and enhancement. This ongoing commitment to improvement is a testament to both Grit and grace.

One of the most critical aspects addressed in the mission's overhaul was the landing system. The new design incorporated self-leveling feet with enhanced impact capacity. These remarkable feats of engineering ensured that the lander could withstand the shock of free-falling from a few kilometers above the moon's surface without sustaining damage. This was a pivotal moment in the Chandrayaan-3 mission's journey towards success. The lesson here is clear: Resilience in the face of adversity and the ability to bounce back from setbacks are key components of Grit and grace. Life, much like space exploration, is filled with unexpected challenges. Having the fortitude to withstand these challenges and emerge stronger on the other side is a hallmark of personal and professional growth.

ISRO's journey towards Chandrayaan-3 also involved a reevaluation of its communication infrastructure. Recognizing the potential for communication failures, they implemented a more robust communication bridge. This ensured that even in the event of a failure, mission control would maintain contact with the spacecraft. This was yet another example of ISRO's dedication to building redundancy and resilience into their systems. In our own lives, effective communication is paramount. Whether it's in our professional relationships or personal ones, being prepared for potential communication breakdowns can prevent misunderstandings and conflicts. It's a testament to the grace of effective communication and the grit to ensure it remains intact.

The journey from Chandrayaan-2 in 2019 to Chandrayaan-3 in 2023 was a testament to ISRO's unwavering determination and commitment to excellence. It was a journey defined by Grit and grace at every step.

With valuable lessons learned from their past failure, ISRO's Chandrayaan-3 mission was nothing short of extraordinary. On a clear night in January 2023, the world once again held its breath as the Chandrayaan-3 spacecraft descended towards the moon's south pole. This time, the outcome was different. The lander touched down gently on the lunar surface, and the Pragyan rover rolled out to begin its scientific exploration. ISRO had achieved what many thought was impossible. They had become the first space agency to successfully land on the challenging terrain of the moon's south pole. The journey from failure to success was a testament to the power of perseverance, resilience, and adaptability - the embodiment of Grit and grace.

As young professionals, there is much we can learn from ISRO's remarkable journey:

- Embrace Failure with Grace: Failure is not a reflection of your worth or abilities. It's an opportunity to learn and grow. Embrace failure with grace, and use it as a stepping stone towards future success.
- Build Redundancy: In both personal and professional endeavours, consider backup plans and redundancy. Being prepared for unexpected challenges can make a significant difference in achieving your goals.
- Continuous Improvement: Just like ISRO constantly refined their mission, seek opportunities for improvement in your work and life. Never settle for the status quo; strive for excellence.
- Resilience in the Face of Adversity: Life is filled with challenges. The ability to bounce back and overcome setbacks is a testament to your resilience and inner strength.
- Effective Communication: Invest in effective communication. It's the bridge that connects you with others and ensures clarity in your interactions, both professionally and personally.

ISRO's journey from failure to success is a shining example of Grit and grace in action. It reminds us that with determination, humility, and the willingness to learn from our mistakes, we can achieve the seemingly impossible. So, as you embark on your own professional and personal endeavours, remember the lessons from ISRO's Chandrayaan-2 and Chandrayaan-3 missions, and let Grit and grace guide your way to greatness.

V

"The Odyssey of Mindset Mastery"

Unleashing the Power Within

Once upon a time, in the quaint village of Sambhav Nagar, where dreams whispered through the rustling leaves of ancient oak trees, there lived two friends - Jeet and Preet. They were like two peas in a pod, sharing everything from secrets to dreams. Their friendship was a beautiful blend of Grit and grace, a testament to the resilience of the human spirit. One sunny afternoon, while sitting under the shade of the old oak tree that stood at the heart of their village, they stumbled upon a dusty old book titled "Mindset Mastery: Unleashing Your Inner Potential." Little did they know that this book would set them on a transformative journey, a journey filled with trials and triumphs that would forever change their lives.

The Seed of Curiosity: A New Beginning

As Jeet and Preet pored over the pages of the book, they were introduced to a concept that would become their guiding star - the growth mindset. It was as if a hidden door to a world of possibilities had swung open before them. The idea that their abilities and intelligence were not fixed traits but rather something that could be developed with effort and learning fascinated them. This newfound understanding was the first chapter in their story of Grit and grace. They began to see their challenges not as dead ends but as stepping stones to growth. Their dreams, once shrouded in doubt, now gleamed with possibility. The spark of curiosity had been ignited, and they were eager to set forth on their adventure.

Confronting Limiting Beliefs: The Cave of Reflection; With newfound enthusiasm, Jeet and Preet realized that they needed to confront their limiting beliefs - those sneaky voices in their heads that whispered doubts and fears. Jeet, who had always dreamt of becoming an artist, had convinced himself that he was "not creative enough." Preet, an aspiring writer, believed she was "not talented enough" to ever be published. These self-imposed limitations were the dragons they had to slay to continue their journey of Grit and grace. In the heart of the forest, they stumbled upon the legendary Cave of Reflection. It was said that anyone who entered the cave would be faced with their deepest fears and doubts. Armed with determination, they ventured in. Shadows danced on the cave walls, embodying their fears. Through tearful conversations and shared realizations, they understood that these beliefs were mere illusions they had allowed to hold them back. Emerging from the cave, Jeet and Preet felt lighter, as if a weight had been lifted from their shoulders. They had stared into the abyss of their doubts and emerged stronger. They knew that overcoming limiting beliefs was an ongoing process, so they decided to cultivate a garden of optimism within their minds. This garden, nurtured by Grit & Grace, would become their sanctuary.

Cultivating the Garden of Optimism: A Continuous Practice; As they tended to their mental garden, they discovered that a shift in mindset was not just a one-time event but a continuous practice. It required patience, self-compassion, and a daily commitment to nurturing positive thoughts. They watered it with positive affirmations and fertilized it with self-compassion. This garden was a testament to their resilience, a place where Grit and grace flourished.

As autumn leaves rustled underfoot, the duo stumbled upon a puzzle in the meadow. Each piece bore a challenge they had faced - big or small. As they solved the puzzle, they realized that their growth mindset was the key to their success. It was their proactive approach to challenges that allowed them to piece together the puzzle of their dreams. Rather than waiting for solutions, they had become the architects of their fate.

Sharing the Wisdom: The Mindset Fair; The word of Jeet and Preet's transformation spread like wildfire through Sambhav Nagar. Friends and neighbors were inspired by their journey. The duo decided to share their newfound wisdom by hosting a village-wide "Mindset Fair." People from all walks of life came to learn about shifting their mindset, letting go of limiting beliefs and embracing challenges. The fair became a celebration of growth, resilience, and the power of the human spirit. It was a testament to the enduring theme of Grit and grace that had guided them through their odyssey.

The Winter of Uncertainty: Embracing the Unknown; As winter snow blanketed Sambhav Nagar, Jeet and Preet realized that their journey was far from over. The growth mindset was not a destination but a lifelong adventure. With open hearts, they embraced the unknown, ready to face new challenges, explore uncharted territories, and continually expand their horizons. The winter symbolized a period of rest and reflection, a time to gather strength for the next chapter in their tale of Grit and grace.

Reframe the conversation you have with yourself because your word creates your belief if you knowingly and unknowingly self-sabotage yourself just to sound not overtly boastful and over-confident. You need to reflect on your choice of words. Read the below example to reframe your self-talk.

> “*Fixed Mindset: "I can't be a successful artist, I don't have the talent."*
>
> *Growth Mindset: "While I may not possess natural talent, I am determined to put in dedicated effort and cultivate my skills to achieve success as an artist."*”

> “*Fixed Mindset: "I can't be successful in my career, I don't have the connections."*
>
> *Growth Mindset: "Though I may lack existing connections, I am enthusiastic about building a strong network and nurturing relationships to propel my career forward."*”

> “*Fixed Mindset: "I can't be a good athlete, I am not tall enough."*

Growth Mindset: "Even though I might not have the ideal height, my commitment to hard work and skill development will pave the way for me to excel as an athlete.""

In a lush, sprawling forest lived a baby elephant named Appu. As a curious and spirited calf, Appu had a strong penchant for wandering and exploring every nook and cranny of his habitat. Concerned for his safety, the caretakers devised a plan to keep Appu close by—they attached a small, sturdy rope to one of his legs, securing it to a sturdy stomp nearby. As the days turned into months and months into years, Appu grew larger and more robust. The rope, once a powerful deterrent, became a mere thread incapable of restraining his immense strength. However, a remarkable transformation had occurred within Appu's mind. He had unknowingly accepted his limitations, conditioned by the experiences of his past. One day, an opportunity for freedom presented itself. Appu noticed the thin rope still tethered to his leg and the weathered stomp it was attached to. He hesitated his memories of countless attempts to break free flooding his thoughts. But something inside him had changed—he realized that he had outgrown the challenges of his past. With a surge of newfound determination, Appu tugged at the rope, and to his astonishment, it snapped effortlessly.

In that transformative moment, Appu's understanding of his own strength expanded beyond the confines of his history. Not stopping at the rope, he gazed at the ancient trees surrounding him. The idea that once seemed ludicrous now ignited a spark within him. He approached a massive, deeply rooted tree and with sheer power and will, he began to pull. Slowly and steadily, the colossal tree budged, its roots relinquishing their grip on the earth. Appu's persistence and newfound realization had enabled him to accomplish the seemingly impossible. As Appu stood there, triumphant, and free, he became a living testament to the message that transcended his story—a message that whispers to us all: "Do not be confined by the boundaries of your past experiences. Just as the baby elephant grew into a mighty force, you too have evolved and become more powerful than you once believed. With determination and unwavering resolve, even the most deeply rooted challenges can be uprooted, allowing you to reach heights you never thought possible."

And so, dear reader, as the seasons changed, Jeet and Preet's mindset continued to evolve. Their story became a testament to the incredible power of the mind - a power that resides within each and every one of us. Just like them, you too can embark on a journey of mindset mastery. You can rewrite the narratives that hold you back, nurture the seeds of optimism, and sculpt a mindset that thrives on challenges.

> “*"The greatest discovery of all time is that a person can change his future by merely changing his attitude." - Oprah Winfrey*”

" Unleashing Potential: Lessons from the Shark Tank ?"

In a captivating experiment, a marine biologist orchestrated a thought-provoking scenario that revealed profound insights into human behaviour through the lens of a shark's experience. Within the confines of a research endeavour, a shark found itself within a spacious holding tank alongside a group of enticing bait fish. Naturally, the shark wasted no time in pursuing its instincts, darting through the water with precision to seize and consume the smaller fish. The initial outcome aligned with expectations – a classic predator-prey interaction.

However, the narrative took an intriguing turn as the marine biologist introduced an ingenious element: a sturdy sheet of transparent fiberglass. This simple addition partitioned the tank into distinct territories. On one side rested the formidable shark, on the other, a fresh congregation of bait fish.

Upon launching into attack mode once more, the shark's determination was met with an unexpected force – the fiberglass barrier. The collision was a startling revelation, leaving the shark momentarily stunned. Unperturbed, the creature repeatedly attempted its aggressive advances, yet the barrier remained insurmountable. The contrast between its efforts and the unscathed bait fish in the adjacent partition became increasingly conspicuous.

As time elapsed, a fascinating transformation unfolded. The shark's once fervent assaults dwindled in frequency and intensity. Persistence gave way to resignation, and its attempts at conquering the barrier diminished. Weeks of repetitions etched a powerful lesson into the shark's behaviour – the belief that a formidable divide lay between it and the tantalizing prey.

Then came the pivotal moment. The marine biologist chose to dismantle the fibreglass barricade, presenting an unobstructed path to the bait fish. An astonishing revelation followed: the shark refrained from launching an attack. The psychological barrier, meticulously crafted through past experiences, wielded more control than any physical obstacle. The bait fish roamed freely, unthreatened by the once fearsome predator. The allegory's resonance with our lives is undeniable. Our journeys are rife with setbacks and frustrations. In the wake of these challenges, it's all too easy to succumb to self-doubt and abandon our pursuits. Like the shark, we can become entrapped by an illusionary barrier, convinced that our previous failures dictate a future of futility.

The essence of the narrative underscores the power of the mind in shaping our trajectories. Just as the shark's mindset was moulded by repeated encounters with the fibreglass, our beliefs about our potential can be heavily influenced by our past experiences. It serves as a reminder that true barriers are often conjured within our minds, limiting us far more than any external circumstances.

The story of the shark in the tank invites us to reflect on our narratives. It urges us to challenge the mental partitions we've erected, fueled by past letdowns. By recognizing the influence of our thoughts and acknowledging our capacity to transcend self-imposed barriers, we can redefine our paths and chart a course toward unexplored possibilities."

Remember, the story of your mindset is a story only you can write. Will you choose to embrace a growth mindset and unearth your hidden potential? Will you challenge the beliefs that confine you and create a life that blooms with possibilities? The choice is yours, and the adventure awaits. So, my friend, are you ready to dive into the depths of your own mind and emerge as the author of your destiny? The pen is in your hand, and the pages of your mindset are waiting to be filled with the ink of possibility.

Mastering the Mindset: Kobe Bryant's Blueprint for Exceptional Success

Picture this: a young Kobe Bryant, a force of nature on the basketball court, but what truly set him apart wasn't just his incredible talent. It was his mindset mastery and relentless work ethic that transformed him into a legend. Let's dive into the story of how Kobe conquered the game and our hearts with a determination that resonates with each of us, teaching us that success is earned, not given.

He would not be outworked Imagine facing off against the Lakers, knowing Kobe was on the other side. Jay Williams, a fellow player, decided to outsmart Kobe by arriving at the court early to prepare. But guess what? Kobe was already there, drenched in sweat, putting in the hours. He had been grinding for over an hour before anyone else showed up. Jay couldn't believe his eyes as he watched Kobe give his all for another half-hour.

The outcome? The Lakers emerged victorious, with Kobe scoring a whopping 40 points. Jay, curious about Kobe's dedication, questioned him afterwards. Kobe's response was a mic-drop moment: "Because I saw you there. I saw you come in and wanted you to know that it doesn't matter how hard you work, I'm willing to work harder than you." That's the kind of mindset mastery that turned Kobe into an unstoppable force.

He was the first to arrive and the last to leave Kobe wasn't just about the glitz and glamour of the game day. He was the embodiment of commitment, the early bird catching not just the worm but the whole feast. He would show up for a 7 a.m. practice at 5 a.m. That's dedication in action. After high school practice, while others were winding down, he was making his teammates stay for grueling one-on-one games. Even before the official practice started, he'd be in the gym, sweating and honing his skills. This wasn't just routine; it was a declaration that he was willing to outwork anyone, including the best of the best. Remember the lead-up to the 2008 Olympics? While most were still rubbing the sleep from their eyes, Kobe was already three hours deep into his workout. Chris Bosh and Dwayne Wade, two top-tier players themselves, were left awestruck by his dedication. Kobe's secret? He trained four times more than others. His day began at 3 a.m., and he pushed through multiple training sessions until 9 p.m. That's what set him apart.

Kobe trained 4x more; Kobe's equation for success was simple: practice plus practice equals mastery. He understood that if he wanted to be the best, he couldn't settle for mediocrity. "If your job is to be the best basketball player in the world," he explained, "you have to practice." His routine was anything but ordinary. He trained at the crack of dawn, allowing his body to recover before diving in again. His sessions weren't limited to two; he rocked four intense workouts daily. He knew that this was the path to greatness, the blueprint that would separate him from the crowd.

As he shared, "I start my day early because I can get more work in." He wasn't just relying on talent; he was investing in sweat equity. And that investment paid off, propelling him to the top of the basketball world.

His fulfilment came from pushing daily to reach his full potential; Kobe's journey wasn't a stroll in the park; it was a relentless pursuit of excellence. During his retirement ceremony, he revealed the core of his success: "It is in those times when you get up early and you work hard... You don't want to push yourself, but you do it anyway. That is the dream." The dream wasn't just about the destination; it was about every step, and every challenge overcome. It was about embracing the grind and finding joy in the process. Champions are made of these moments—those early mornings, those late nights, the times when doubts creep in but are crushed by determination. Dale Carnegie's wisdom echoed in Kobe's actions: "The thing is to get the work done." Kobe believed in his journey, and that belief fueled his relentless pursuit of greatness.

Kobe Bryant's story isn't just about basketball; it's a universal tale of how mastering your mindset and embracing hard work can elevate you to extraordinary heights. So, as you face your challenges, remember Kobe's legacy. The sweat, the sacrifice, the unyielding dedication—it all adds up to a life lived without regrets, a life that echoes his words: "Today is the tomorrow you worried about yesterday."

In this chapter, we embarked on a captivating journey with Jeet and Preet, two friends from Sambhav Nagar, as they discovered the transformative power of mindset. Through their adventures, we learned about the growth mindset, the importance of confronting limiting beliefs, and the continuous practice of cultivating optimism. We also explored the inspiring tale of Appu, the baby elephant, who broke free from the mental barriers that had held him back for years. Lastly, we delved into Kobe Bryant's remarkable dedication and mindset mastery, which propelled him to legendary status.

Key Takeaways

Growth Mindset: Embrace the belief that your abilities and intelligence can be developed with effort and learning. Challenges are opportunities for growth, not roadblocks.

Confront Limiting Beliefs: Challenge the doubts and fears that hold you back. Just as Jeet and Preet faced their inner demons, you can too.

Cultivate Optimism: Nurture a mindset that thrives on challenges. Your mental garden needs daily care, with positive affirmations and self-compassion as essential tools.

Break Free from Mental Barriers: Like Appu, recognize that you've outgrown the limitations of your past experiences. You have the power to uproot self-imposed barriers.

Dedication and Work Ethic: Kobe Bryant's story emphasizes that talent alone is not enough. Dedication, hard work, and a willingness to outwork others are essential ingredients for success.

The Joy of the Journey: Find fulfilment in the process, not just the destination. Embrace the grind, persevere through challenges, and savor every step of your journey.

In the chapters of our protagonists' lives, we've uncovered the timeless truths of mindset mastery, resilience, and determination. The stories of Jeet and Preet, Appu the Baby Elephant, and Kobe Bryant all share a common thread—Grit and grace.

As you close this chapter and carry these lessons with you, remember that your life's story is a narrative that only you can write. Embrace a growth mindset, confront your limiting beliefs, and cultivate optimism in your mental garden. Break free from the barriers that hold you back and let your dedication and work ethic be your guiding stars. In the grand tapestry of your life, find joy in every moment of your journey, for it is in these moments that you'll discover the true power within you. As you turn the page to the next chapter, do so with confidence and the unwavering belief that you can shape your destiny through the mastery of your mindset. The adventure continues, and the possibilities are limitless.

"The only limit to our realization of tomorrow will be our doubts of today." - Franklin D. Roosevelt"

VI

"Science Of Stress Bursting"

Unveiling the Secrets of Stress Management

In the hustle and bustle of our lives, stress comes knocking in various forms. It's like a puzzle with different pieces - some from our interactions with others, some from within ourselves, and some from the world around us. When stress barges in uninvited, it's as if our body and mind stage a grand performance, a symphony of sensations and emotions. Imagine it as a magic show where stress disguises itself as physical experiences: aching muscles, pounding headaches, a vanishing appetite, a racing heart like a sports car, skyrocketing blood pressure, overwhelming fatigue, that pesky companion named anxiety, and a drifting focus like a runaway balloon. But here's the intriguing part: these sensations aren't chaos; they're our body's survival tools, gifts handed down by our ancestors. It's as if our body shouts, "Time for 'fight or flight' mode!" When stress arrives, our body transforms into a superhero, muscles tensing up, preparing for action, and rerouting blood to vital areas, charging them up. But there's a catch. While we're all set to tackle immediate threats, our body hits the snooze button on things like digestion and immune defenses.

This sneak peek into the enigmatic world of stress is what sometimes makes us feel unwell after spending too much time in its company. It's as if stress hangs up a sign that reads, "Welcome, Chronic Diseases!" That's why it's crucial to become a detective and figure out what's causing your stress. If you can dodge those stress triggers, fantastic! If not, don't fret—there's a backup plan. You can learn tricks to deal with stress, like giving it a friendly nod and embracing a more relaxed lifestyle. That means hanging out with mindfulness, kicking back with relaxation, and having a chat with meditation.

Imagine stress as a mystery novel, and you're both the reader and the hero. The clues are your body's signals, and the adventure is discovering how to handle stress like a pro. It's a journey where science meets your everyday life, guiding you to be pals with stress instead of letting it steal the show.

> “*"The greatest weapon against stress is our ability to choose one thought over another."* - *William James*”

Embarking on a Quest for Calm: Exploring the Secrets of Beating Stress

Amidst the chaos of India's bustling streets and the relentless demands of daily life, there exists a path less taken—a path that promises inner peace. Picture a world where stressors lose their grip, where calmness reigns, and where self-care becomes your sanctuary. This journey is not just worth taking; it's essential. In this tale, we delve into the art of managing stress, guided by the magic of mindfulness, meditation, and relaxation techniques. With science as our ally and inspiring stories of Indian luminaries as our compass, let's embark on this transformative adventure.

The Magic of Mindfulness

Close your eyes and envision a tiny Himalayan village. In this serene haven lived Rajiv, a farmer who exuded unusual tranquility. He held the secret of mindfulness—a practice of being fully present in each moment. Science confirms Rajiv's wisdom; studies reveal that mindfulness reduces cortisol, the notorious stress hormone, and enhances cognitive function. Clinical trials align with Rajiv's teachings. Participants who embraced mindfulness reported diminished anxiety and improved emotional regulation. By immersing themselves in simple acts such as conscious breathing and mindful tasks, they erected a protective shield against stress.

Meditation

A Journey Within; In the soft glow of dawn, Anjali, a renowned actress, found solace in meditation. With every breath, she peeled away layers of stress, unveiling a serene core. Science, too, stands as a testament to the power of meditation, showing that it strengthens brain regions associated with emotional resilience. Clinical experiments conducted at Bangalore's National Institute of Mental Health and Neurosciences corroborate meditation's efficacy. Frequent meditation practitioners exhibited brainwave patterns indicative of enhanced emotional strength. This ancient practice proves itself timeless and indispensable in the modern world.

Relaxation Techniques - A Calming Dance

In the heart of Delhi's frenetic pace, Ramesh, a thriving entrepreneur, discovered solace in relaxation exercises. These seemingly simple yet profoundly effective tools, including deep breathing, muscle relaxation, and visualization of tranquil scenes, whisked away stress like leaves carried by the wind. Clinical studies provide concrete evidence of relaxation's benefits. Individuals who embraced relaxation techniques reported slower heartbeats, reduced blood pressure, and improved sleep quality. These practices rewired the body's response to stress, restoring a harmonious balance.

> “*"Stress is an alarm clock that lets you know you're attached to something that's not true for you." - Byron Katie*”

Crafting a Symphony of Self-Care

Amidst the vibrant tapestry of India's entertainment industry, Kavya, a celebrated singer, emerged as a self-care ambassador. Amidst rehearsals, performances, and the dazzle of the spotlight, she prioritized her well-being with unwavering dedication. Science echoes Kavya's approach; research underscores that a holistic self-care regimen elevates happiness and nurtures resilience. Clinical assessments further validate the significance of self-care. Individuals who invested time in self-care experienced reduced stress levels and greater overall life satisfaction. This routine became a symphony that played in harmony with life's frenetic rhythm, demonstrating its transformative power. As we journey through the labyrinth of stress management, guided by mindfulness, meditation, and relaxation exercises, we weave a narrative of victory. From the serene Himalayan village to the bustling urban streets and the glittering lights of fame, we discover that stress can be tamed and transformed. Science lends its support to these ancient practices, unravelling the intricate shifts within the body that lead to serenity.

Let us draw inspiration from Rajiv's mindfulness, Anjali's meditation, Ramesh's relaxation techniques, and Kavya's self-care regimen. Their stories guide us to a realm where stress holds no dominion, where the melody of well-being plays continuously, and where each day becomes a canvas for self-discovery and tranquillity. The journey is ours to undertake—a path leading to inner serenity.

> “*"The deeper the feeling of being overwhelmed, the greater the urgency to slow down and take a look at what's behind it." - Carl Honore"*
> ”

In Conclusion

In our modern lives, where stress often seems like an unwelcome guest, we have the power to change our relationship with it. By embracing the principles of mindfulness, meditation, relaxation, and self-care, we can transform stress from a villain into a companion on our journey towards inner peace and well-being. Grit and grace are the cornerstones of this transformation. Grit represents our determination to confront stress head-on, to learn its secrets, and to adapt. Grace embodies the serenity and self-compassion needed to navigate life's challenges with resilience and poise.

As young professionals, you have the opportunity to embark on this journey of self-discovery and stress management. Through mindfulness, meditation, relaxation, and self-care, you can create a life that is not just about surviving but thriving. The stories of Rajiv, Anjali, Ramesh, and Kavya serve as beacons of hope and inspiration, reminding us that the path to inner peace is within our reach.

So, as you navigate the maze of daily life, remember the power of Grit and grace. Embrace stress as a teacher rather than a tormentor, and let it guide you towards a life filled with calmness, resilience, and well-being. The journey is yours to take, and the destination is a life where stress no longer holds sway, where you become the master of your emotions, and where every day is an opportunity to grow and flourish.

Key Takeaways

- Stress comes in various forms but understanding its physical and emotional manifestations is the first step in managing it effectively.
- Stress is a natural response designed to prepare us for action, but chronic stress can lead to health problems, making it essential to identify and manage its triggers.
- Mindfulness, the practice of being fully present in the moment, can reduce stress by lowering cortisol levels and improving emotional control.
- Meditation strengthens brain regions associated with emotional resilience, making it a valuable tool for managing stress in our modern world.
- Relaxation techniques, such as deep breathing and muscle relaxation, can lower heart rate and blood pressure, promoting a balanced stress response.
- Self-care is a symphony that plays alongside life's demands, enhancing happiness and resilience while

reducing stress levels.

- Grit and grace are essential qualities in the journey to manage stress effectively. Grit represents determination and resilience, while Grace embodies serenity and self-compassion.
- Stress can be transformed from a foe into a companion on the path to inner peace and well-being.
- Embrace stress as a teacher, learn its secrets, and use mindfulness, meditation, relaxation, and self-care to thrive in your daily life.
- Your journey towards stress management and well-being is a personal one, and the destination is a life where you are the master of your emotions, resilient in the face of challenges, and at peace with yourself.

VII

"Building Strong Relationships"

Nurturing Meaningful Connections

In the hustle and bustle of our daily lives, there's an intricate tapestry being woven, a tapestry that holds together the very essence of who we are. This tapestry is made up of relationships, those vibrant threads that intertwine our experiences, emotions, and personal growth. Whether we realize it or not, we all need a network of support during the turbulent times that life throws our way. It's in these moments of struggle that we truly appreciate the value of relationships and the profound impact they can have on our lives. Welcome to the world of 'Grit & Grace': a journey through the art of building strong relationships and nurturing connections that resonate deeply.

The Essence of Strong Relationships: Trust, Communication, and Mutual Understanding

Imagine your relationships as delicate blossoms in the garden of life. Each one is unique, each one demanding nurturing care and attention. Just as a plant needs sunlight, water, and fertile soil to flourish, relationships thrive on trust, communication, and mutual understanding.

Trust - The Cornerstone of Connection

Trust is the very cornerstone that upholds the structure of any connection. It's the bridge that allows individuals to cross the chasm of vulnerability, knowing that their emotions and vulnerabilities are safe in the hands of their loved ones. Without trust, relationships wither, unable to withstand the storms that life inevitably throws at us. Think of trust as the 'grit' in your relationships, that solid foundation on which everything else is built. It's not just about believing someone won't betray you; it's also about having faith in their intentions, and in their ability to support and understand you.

Communication - The Gentle Breeze of Connection

Communication, like the gentle breeze that carries fragrance across the garden, breathes life into relationships. Effective communication isn't just about speaking; it's about truly listening, allowing each person's thoughts and feelings to be acknowledged and validated. In today's world, dominated by digital exchanges and quick text messages, genuine conversations have become a rarity. We've lost touch with the 'grace' of real communication. Rediscovering this art is pivotal in forging relationships that resonate deeply. When we talk about 'grace' in communication, we mean the ability to convey your thoughts and emotions with empathy, kindness, and clarity. It's the 'grace' of choosing your words thoughtfully, ensuring they land softly on the ears of your loved ones, making them feel understood and cherished.

Life is a rollercoaster, marked by peaks of joy and valleys of despair. In these valleys, the presence of strong relationships and social support becomes a beacon of light. Social support encompasses emotional, practical, and even informational assistance that we receive from others. It acts as a safety net that catches us when we stumble and provides the reassurance that we are not alone in our struggles.

During tough times, the warmth of a friend's embrace or a family member's comforting words can provide solace that no amount of solitude can replicate. Research has shown that social support not only alleviates emotional distress but also contributes to physical well-being. The power of human connection is such that it can lower stress hormones, boost immunity, and accelerate healing. In a world that sometimes feels chaotic and harsh, these connections embody the 'grit & grace' of life itself. They are the sturdy pillars that hold us up when life's storms threaten to knock us down. now, let's talk about nurturing these connections, about weaving 'grit & grace' into the fabric of our relationships. In a world that often encourages superficial interactions, the journey towards depth and authenticity demands conscious effort.

Vulnerability

Vulnerability is the key that unlocks the doors to profound connections. It's the 'grace' to let others see us as we truly are, imperfections and all. This act of courage fosters intimacy. When we share our genuine selves, we invite others to do the same, creating an environment of mutual openness and acceptance. Creating shared experiences adds layers of depth to relationships. Engaging in activities together, whether it's cooking a meal, embarking on a hike, or pursuing a common hobby, creates memories that form the bedrock of a lasting bond. Just as a tree's rings tell the story of its growth, shared experiences become chapters in the story of our relationships. These shared experiences are the 'grit' of your connection. They're the experiences that you can look back on, the memories that remind you of the beautiful journey you've undertaken together.

Conflict and Change - The Tests of Resilience

Relationships, like life itself, are in a constant state of evolution. As we navigate the twists and turns, we must embrace change while nurturing the roots that hold our connections firm. Sometimes, conflicts arise, and misunderstandings cast shadows over our bonds. In these moments, the gentle touch of empathy can mend what is broken. Conflict is an inevitable part of life, but it doesn't have to be the end of a relationship. It can often be an opportunity for growth and deeper understanding. It's the 'grace' to acknowledge differences and work through them, and the 'grit' to emerge on the other side, stronger and more united.

Resilience - The Unbreakable Bond

Resilience is the golden thread that runs through the fabric of strong relationships. It is the ability to face challenges, adapt, and emerge stronger, individually and as a unit. Resilience is not the absence of struggle, but the capacity to face adversity hand-in-hand, knowing that the bond forged through trials is unbreakable. Think of resilience as the 'grit & grace' that helps your relationship weather the storms of life. It's the determination to keep going, to keep growing, even when the world seems against you.

In the symphony of life, relationships compose the most melodious notes, harmonizing our joys and consoling our sorrows. Building strong relationships and fostering meaningful connections is an art that requires patience, effort, and a genuine heart. As we traverse the landscape of existence, let us remember that the connections we cultivate are the true treasures that enrich our journey. May we approach each relationship with the tenderness of a gardener, tending to the seeds of trust, watering the roots of understanding, and watching with awe as the blossoms of connection unfold in all their splendour.

Effective Communication and Conflict Resolution

Now, as we continue our journey through the world of 'Grit and grace,' we delve into the significance of communication skills and conflict resolution strategies, understanding how they enhance both personal and professional relationships. Picture communication as a bridge connecting hearts and minds, allowing thoughts and emotions to flow freely. However, this bridge can become rickety without proper care and maintenance. Developing strong communication skills is like reinforcing that bridge, ensuring a smooth and steady passage of understanding between individuals.

Active Listening - The Heartbeat of Connection

Active listening is the cornerstone of effective communication. Often, we find ourselves formulating responses before the other person has even finished speaking. True listening involves suspending judgment and immersing ourselves in their words, seeking to grasp not only the content but the emotions and intentions behind them. This practice fosters empathy, deepening the connection between speaker and listener. Imagine this as the 'grace' in your conversations. It's the art of truly hearing someone, not just their words but also their feelings and intentions. It's about making them feel valued and understood.

Expressing Ourselves - The Power of Words

Expressing ourselves clearly is equally crucial. Just as a painter uses precise brushstrokes to convey meaning, our words should be chosen thoughtfully to convey our thoughts and emotions accurately. Clarity in expression prevents misunderstandings, building a foundation of trust and comprehension. When we talk about 'grace' in expression, we mean the ability to convey your thoughts and feelings with kindness and empathy. It's about using words that heal, not harm, words that build bridges, not walls.

Conflict Resolution Strategies

In the vast ocean of relationships, storms of conflict are inevitable. Yet, these storms need not capsize the ship of connection. Conflict, when managed with finesse, can lead to stronger ties and deeper understanding. Effective conflict resolution strategies are the compass that guides us through these tempests, steering us toward calmer waters. Approaching conflicts with an open heart and a willingness to understand is paramount. Instead of viewing conflicts as battles to be won, consider them as opportunities to learn and grow. Listening to the other person's perspective, even if it diverges from our own, lays the groundwork for finding common ground.

Empathy

Empathy is the North Star in conflict resolution. Striving to see the situation from the other person's point of view can transform adversaries into allies. When we understand the underlying emotions and concerns, we can address them with sensitivity, diffusing tension and paving the way for resolution.

Collaborative Problem-Solving

Collaborative problem-solving is the anchor that stabilizes relationships during times of conflict. Working together to find solutions that accommodate both parties' needs fosters a sense of teamwork and shared commitment. Just as a ship emerges stronger from navigating rough waters, relationships can thrive when conflict is addressed constructively. Imagine conflict resolution as the 'grace & grit' in your relationship toolkit. It's the ability to navigate challenges with empathy and determination, to find solutions that strengthen rather than weaken your bond.

Fostering Connections: Personal and Professional

The tapestry of relationships spans both personal and professional realms. In both spheres, effective communication and conflict resolution are indispensable tools for nurturing meaningful connections. In personal relationships, communication enriches the bonds we share with family and friends. Transparent conversations allow for emotional intimacy, enabling us to celebrate each other's joys and provide support during challenges. Conflict resolution strategies help mend rifts, preserving the fabric of these connections through thick and thin. These personal connections are the 'grace' in your life. They're the ones who know your quirks, your dreams, and your flaws, and they love you for all of it.

In the professional arena, communication skills set the stage for collaboration and success. Articulating ideas clearly to colleagues and superiors fosters a productive work environment. When conflicts arise among team members, the ability to address them openly and respectfully prevents disruptions and paves the way for innovation. Think of your professional relationships as the 'grit' that propels your career forward. They're the connections that open doors, inspire innovation, and help you reach new heights in your chosen field.

Conclusion: Crafting Relationships with 'Grit & Grace

As we wrap ourselves in the quilt of life, relationships form the threads that keep us warm and connected. Just as a skilled seamstress weaves intricate patterns, we can cultivate strong connections by honing our communication skills and conflict resolution strategies. In the symphony of communication, let us be both conductor and listener, ensuring that the notes we exchange create harmonies that resonate in the hearts of those we touch. In the face of conflict, let us be navigators, steering our relationships through stormy seas toward the shores of understanding. Through these efforts, we craft relationships that stand the test of time, enriching our personal and professional lives with depth, empathy, and enduring connection.

So, young professionals, as you embark on your journey through the intricate tapestry of life, remember the importance of 'Grit and grace' in your relationships. Trust, communication, vulnerability, shared experiences, conflict resolution, and resilience – these are the tools that will help you weave strong bonds and nurture connections that resonate deeply. In a world that sometimes feels fast-paced and disconnected, these are the qualities that will set you apart and make your relationships truly meaningful. And always keep in mind that the most beautiful tapestries are those that tell stories of 'Grit and grace,' stories of challenges faced and conquered, stories of love, understanding, and enduring connection. So, go out there and craft your masterpiece of relationships, one 'grit & grace' thread at a time.

Key Takeaways

- **Trust is the Cornerstone**: Trust forms the solid foundation of any relationship. It's the 'grit' that holds everything together. Building trust takes time and consistency, but it's essential for connections that stand the test of time.
- **Communication is Vital:** Effective communication is the 'grace' that breathes life into relationships. Active listening, clear expression, and empathetic communication are keys to fostering deeper connections.
- **Vulnerability Strengthens Bonds:** Being open and vulnerable is an act of courage that fosters intimacy and 'grace' in relationships. When you share your genuine self, you invite others to do the same.
- **Shared Experiences Create Depth**: Creating shared experiences adds layers of depth to relationships. These experiences become the 'grit' of your connection, forming lasting memories and stronger bonds.
- **Conflict Can Lead to Growth**: Conflict is inevitable, but it doesn't have to be destructive. Approaching conflicts with empathy, collaborative problem-solving, and a willingness to understand can strengthen relationships.
- **Resilience is Key:** Resilience, the ability to face challenges and emerge stronger, is the 'grit & grace' that keeps relationships thriving. It's about navigating life's ups and downs together, knowing that your bond is unbreakable.
- Apply 'Grit & Grace' in Personal and Professional Life; These principles apply not only to personal relationships but also to your professional life. Effective communication and conflict resolution are valuable tools in both spheres, enriching your personal and career journey.

By embracing these takeaways, you can weave 'Grit and grace' into your relationships, nurturing connections that are profound, enduring, and deeply meaningful.

VIII

"Goal Setting"

Charting Your Path to Success

In the vast tapestry of life, the pursuit of success unfolds as a vibrant, intricate journey. We are the artists of our destinies, wielding the brushes of determination and focus to paint our path to achievement. This chapter is an odyssey into the art of goal setting and accomplishment. It's a journey that takes you through the landscapes of setbacks, the rhythms of motivation, and the kaleidoscope of focus. It's about finding your Grit and grace as a young professional to navigate these terrains with style and substance.

The Significance of Purposeful Goals

Imagine this journey as an expansive canvas waiting for your strokes of brilliance, each brushstroke symbolizing a step towards your aspirations. Purposeful goals are the vibrant palette from which you draw the colors of ambition, each hue representing a different facet of your dreams. They are not just points on your map; they are the guiding stars in your constellation of success. Picture a skilled traveler planning their route meticulously before setting off on an adventure. Similarly, crafting purposeful goals requires a roadmap—a blueprint that outlines the milestones and actions needed to reach your desired destination. Think of the SMART approach as your trusty compass. It helps you set goals that are Specific, Measurable, Achievable, Relevant, and Time-bound, ensuring your expedition is filled with clarity and direction.

Creating Your Trailblazing Roadmap: Artistry in Progress

In the tapestry of your journey, your goals are the destinations you long to explore. Your roadmap, much like a well-planned travel itinerary, charts the course from your current position to your envisioned future. But it's not a rigid blueprint; think of it as a flexible guide that accommodates detours and unexpected vistas. The SMART framework is the artist's palette for your journey. Specificity paints fine lines that define your goals, Measurability adds vivid detail to track your progress, Achievability keeps your feet firmly on the ground, ensuring your goals are attainable, Relevance connects your goals with your values and aspirations, and Time-bound imbues a sense of urgency, akin to the thrill of a limited-time travel offer.

Fueling the Flame of Motivation

As you embark on your journey, motivation becomes your steadfast companion. But, like a flickering flame, it demands care to burn brightly. Cultivating lasting motivation is a journey in itself, requiring you to tend to your mindset, much like a gardener nurturing a garden. Positivity is the sunshine that nourishes your motivation, helping you dispel the clouds of doubt and discouragement. Just as fellow travellers can inspire with their tales, surrounding yourself with supportive individuals adds fuel to your determination. Visualization serves as your postcard from the future, allowing you to experience success before it's even achieved. Celebrating small wins along the way adds vibrant splashes of color to your journey, making the road more joyful.

Transforming Setbacks into Stepping Stones

As you journey towards your goals, setbacks emerge as unexpected roadblocks. But, like seasoned travellers, setbacks are opportunities to explore alternative paths. These challenges aren't dead ends; they are stepping stones on the path to growth and resilience. Resilience becomes your trusty backpack, containing the tools you need to overcome obstacles. Bouncing back from setbacks, much like a traveller adapting to changing conditions, involves integrating the lessons learned into your revised approach. Remember, your journey isn't defined by a single detour; it's defined by your determination to keep moving forward.

Harmonizing Focus and Minimizing Distractions: Navigating the Marketplace of Life

In the bustling marketplace of life, focus is your compass, steering you away from distractions and towards your goals. Distractions, like colorful stalls in a busy bazaar, beckon for your attention. To counter these alluring diversions, mindfulness becomes your shield, helping you stay on track. Just as a traveler breaks their journey into manageable segments, chunking your tasks divides the path to success into achievable steps. This prevents overwhelm and infuses your journey with a sense of accomplishment. Prioritization, akin to selecting must-visit places on a travel itinerary, guides you toward tasks that align with your goals and values.

Nelson Mandela and Apartheid's End in South Africa: A Tale of Grit & Grace

Now, let's delve into the remarkable journey of Nelson Mandela, an icon of setting profound goals and achieving them through resilience, forgiveness, and leadership. His story serves as a beacon of inspiration for young professionals like you, embarking on their quests for success.

Setting Meaningful Goals: Mandela's Vision of a Better South Africa

Mandela's goal was monumental: to dismantle the oppressive system of apartheid in South Africa and establish a society based on equality, justice, and unity. His goal was deeply rooted in his commitment to social justice and his vision of a harmonious nation. It was a purposeful goal that resonated with the hearts of millions. Mandela's path involved years of activism, protest, and negotiations with the government. He emphasized reconciliation and forgiveness as cornerstones for building a new South Africa. His roadmap was a journey filled with sacrifices, including 27 years of imprisonment. But it was a roadmap etched with the unwavering determination to see his vision come to fruition. Mandela's enduring motivation was fueled by his unwavering belief in the power of justice and his dream of a united country. His willingness to endure decades of imprisonment and personal sacrifice demonstrates his exceptional dedication. It was a motivation born from a sense of purpose and an unshakable resolve to see it through.

Mandela faced numerous setbacks, perhaps the most profound being his arrest and imprisonment for 27 years. However, his resilience and commitment to nonviolent resistance allowed him to emerge from prison as a symbol of hope and a catalyst for change. His ability to transform a setback into a stepping stone exemplifies the essence of Grit and grace.

Conclusion: Your Journey Awaits

In the vibrant tapestry of life, setting and achieving goals is the very essence of personal and professional success. You are the artist, blending the colors of determination and focus to create a masterpiece of achievement. With each stroke of resilience, each touch of positivity, and each mindful step, you craft a journey that transcends challenges and arrives at the canvas of success.

As you travel the roads of your aspirations, remember that every goal accomplished is not just a triumph; it's a testament to the artistry of human potential. Just as a traveler returns from their journey with stories to tell, so too will you share tales of your journey—of determination, setbacks, and triumphs. And like the most captivating travel stories, your stories of success will inspire others to set sail on their journeys of achievement. So, young professionals, embrace your Grit and grace, for your canvas of success awaits your bold strokes and vivid colors. Chart your path, set your goals, stay motivated, and navigate the setbacks with resilience. With purposeful goals as your North Star, you'll paint a journey that not only leads to success but leaves a lasting impression on the world. Your odyssey has just begun, and the world eagerly awaits the masterpiece you'll create.

here are six key takeaways from the chapter "Charting Your Path to Personal and Professional Success: Embracing Grit & Grace":

- Purposeful Goals are Your Guiding Stars: Just as skilled traveler plans their journey, purposeful goals serve as your compass on the path to success. They provide direction, focus, and meaning to your endeavors.

- The SMART Framework is Your Artist's Palette: Use Specific, Measurable, Achievable, Relevant, and Time-bound goals as your palette to craft meaningful goals. This framework helps you clarify your objectives and ensures they are attainable.
- Motivation is Your Travel Companion: Cultivate lasting motivation by surrounding yourself with positivity, and supportive individuals, and visualizing your success. Celebrate small wins along the way to keep your motivation burning bright.
- Setbacks are Stepping Stones: Treat setbacks as opportunities for growth and resilience. Embrace challenges with a mindset of learning and adaptability, just like a seasoned traveler navigates unexpected roadblocks.
- Focus is Your Compass: Stay on track by harmonizing focus and minimizing distractions. Chunk your tasks to prevent overwhelm, prioritize your goals, and use mindfulness as a shield against diversions.
- Learn from Nelson Mandela: Nelson Mandela's journey to end apartheid illustrates the power of setting meaningful goals, crafting a dedicated roadmap, maintaining unwavering motivation, and turning setbacks into triumphs. His story embodies the essence of Grit and grace.
- Your Journey Awaits: You are the artist of your journey, and your canvas of success is ready for your bold strokes. Remember that every goal accomplished is a testament to the artistry of human potential, and your stories of determination and triumph will inspire others on their journeys to success. Embrace your Grit and

grace as you embark on this vibrant adventure.

> "*"A winner is a dreamer who never gives up." - Nelson Madela*
> "

IX

"Adversity as Opportunity"

Challenges as Catalysts for Positive Transformation

Adversity, that persistent and unrelenting force in human life, comes in many guises. Personal setbacks, physical limitations, and societal barriers –wrap themselves around us, testing our mettle and pushing us to our limits. It often feels like a storm that can swallow us whole, but throughout history, countless individuals have weathered these tempests and emerged not just intact but transformed. This chapter is an exploration of the incredible stories of individuals like Stephen Hawking, Dr. A. P. J. Abdul Kalam, Narendra Modi, Muniba Mazari, and Sudha Chandran, who embraced adversity as a catalyst for positive change. By diving into their journeys, we unlock profound insights into how challenges can serve as stepping stones to a life imbued with purpose and fulfilment.

Stephen Hawking: The Triumph Over the Physical Abyss

Picture this: a young Stephen Hawking, brilliant and full of promise, suddenly faced with the devastating diagnosis of ALS, a disease that would gradually rob him of his physical abilities. Yet, Hawking did not bow down to despair; instead, he faced adversity head-on. He channelled his energy and intellect into groundbreaking research on the cosmos and the enigmatic world of black holes. With unyielding determination, Hawking not only expanded our understanding of the universe but also became a beacon of inspiration for those grappling with physical limitations. His narrative showcases how adversity can be the spark that ignites a lifelong quest for knowledge and discovery.

Dr. A. P. J. Abdul Kalam: From Poverty to the Pinnacle of Presidency

Dr. A. P. J. Abdul Kalam's story is a testament to the human spirit's boundless resilience. Born into poverty in a small Indian village, Kalam faced adversity early on that could have stifled his dreams. However, he transformed these setbacks into motivation to excel in academics and contribute to India's scientific progress. With an unwavering focus on education and unrelenting hard work, Kalam ascended the ranks of the Indian space and missile programs, eventually reaching the highest office in the land as the President of India. His life illustrates how adversity can kindle the fire of determination, propelling individuals to reach the zenith of their potential.

Narendra Modi: Navigating Political Storms

Narendra Modi, the Prime Minister of India, is no stranger to adversity. His political journey, rife with challenges and controversies, reflects the turbulence of a tempestuous sea. Yet, Modi seized these challenges as opportunities to connect with the masses and enact transformative policies. His resilience in the face of adversity enabled him to rise above criticism and steer his vision for a better India. Modi's story is a powerful reminder of how adversity can be harnessed to forge connections with people, drive change, and triumph over opposition.

Muniba Mazari: The Art of Resilience and Empowerment

Muniba Mazari, an artist, and motivational speaker, rewrote her life's script after a life-altering car accident left her paralyzed from the waist down. Rather than succumbing to the despair and bitterness that such profound adversity could have bred, Mazari channelled her pain into art and advocacy. Through her paintings and public speaking, she inspires others to confront their struggles and redefine their identities. Mazari's story underscores the incredible capacity of creative expression and a positive outlook to emerge from even the darkest adversity.

Sudha Chandran: Rising from the Ashes

Sudha Chandran, a celebrated Bharatanatyam dancer and actress, weaves a tale of resilience that stands shoulder-to-shoulder with the giants of adversity. Her life took an unexpected turn when a car accident led to the amputation of her right leg. In the world of dance, where every movement is a testament to the human body's grace and precision, such a loss could have been utterly devastating. However, Sudha's mindset became her most powerful ally. She envisioned a future where her passion would remain undiminished, and that vision became her guiding star. Her story is a testament to the power of adaptability. Rather than abandoning her passion, Sudha adapted it to her new reality. With the creation of a prosthetic limb, the "Jaipur Foot," she embodied adaptability. Her embrace of change showcased her resilience, allowing her to dance once again and conquer the stage.

Self-compassion was at the core of Sudha's journey. She forgave herself for the accident and transformed her tragedy into an inspiration for millions. Her characters in dance dramas mirrored her triumph over obstacles, and her journey from pain and despair to renewed purpose was an embodiment of her own characters' arcs. Sudha's journey in the entertainment industry underscored the importance of problem-solving skills. Faced with skepticism, she persisted and established herself as a versatile actress. Her ability to find innovative solutions, much like her dance moves, reflected her resilience and determination. Self-care played a vital role in Sudha's life. Balancing rigorous practice with moments of rejuvenation, her practice of yoga and meditation kept her physically and mentally fit. It served as a testament to the importance of self-care in nurturing resilience.

Sudha's support network was an anchor in her life. Her family and mentors bolstered her when she faltered, reflecting the essence of a strong support system. Their unwavering belief in her was a testament to the power of a community that fosters resilience. Adaptability was evident as Sudha transitioned to acting. Her ability to embrace different roles and genres showcased her versatility. Her journey into acting paralleled her journey of resilience—transformative and filled with evolution.

Gratitude was woven into Sudha's every performance. Her dedication was a tribute to her parents, who supported her through her challenges. Her humility reflected her gratitude, reminding us of the importance of acknowledging those who uplift us in our journey. Lastly, her emotional regulation was evident in her every graceful movement. Just as she expressed emotions through dance, she navigated her life's challenges with composure. Her ability to channel her emotions into her art showcased her mastery over both her craft and herself. Sudha Chandran's journey epitomizes resilience in every sense. From a life-changing accident to conquering the stage and screen, her story embodies the essence of resilience strategies—the very strategies that form the heart of this book. Her life is a beacon, illuminating the path for others to navigate their challenges with determination, grace, and an unwavering spirit.

The Science Behind Adversity and Exemplary Success: Unveiling Psychological Transformation

Adversity, that formidable adversary we all face, often serves as the crucible in which exceptional success stories are forged. The scientific reasons underpinning this phenomenon illuminate how adversity shapes our psychology and our approach to life. By unravelling these dynamics, we can glean essential lessons to apply to our journeys, harnessing challenges as catalysts for growth.

Adversity, by its very nature, demands **resilience** – the ability to rebound from setbacks. Researchers have discovered that confronting challenges triggers the brain's stress response, which, when managed effectively, contributes to the cultivation of resilience. This resilience becomes a precious asset, equipping individuals to persevere in the face of future adversities. The brain releases stress hormones like cortisol during adversity and mastering the regulation of these hormones enhances an individual's capacity to cope with stress and emerge stronger.

The brain's astonishing ability to rewire itself, known as **neuroplasticity**, plays a pivotal role in the transformation from adversity to success. When confronted with challenges, the brain adapts by forming new neural pathways. This rewiring often gives rise to a growth mindset – the belief that abilities and intelligence can be developed through effort. By embracing this mindset, individuals harness their brain's plasticity to continuously learn and evolve, turning adversity into a catalyst for self-improvement.

Adversity compels individuals to engage in **adaptive problem-solving.** Overcoming challenges requires creative thinking, innovative strategies, and a willingness to experiment. Neuroscientific studies highlight that tackling complex problems activates regions of the brain associated with decision-making and cognitive flexibility. As individuals consistently confront and conquer challenges, their ability to navigate complexity and find effective solutions becomes honed.

Adversity often triggers intense negative emotions, such as fear, frustration, and sadness. Successful individuals exhibit **higher emotional regulation** – the ability to manage and redirect these emotions constructively. Neuroscientific ally, emotional regulation relies on the prefrontal cortex's control over the amygdala, the brain's emotional center. Through practice, individuals can learn to mitigate the impact of negative emotions, facilitating clearer thinking and better decision-making during challenging times.

Key Takeaways

Embrace a Growth Mindset: Challenges are growth opportunities. See setbacks as temporary hurdles, not permanent limitations, and view them as stepping stones to improvement.

Build Resilience: Develop the capacity to adapt to adversity. Regard setbacks as temporary obstacles and nurture inner strength to persevere in the face of challenges.

Embrace Change: Understand that the brain's plasticity enables adaptation. Welcome change and see adversity as an opportunity to rewire your brain for success.

Practice Emotional Regulation: Learn to manage negative emotions that arise from adversity. By controlling emotional reactions, you can think more clearly and make better decisions.

Foster Innovation: Approach challenges as opportunities to innovate and problem-solve. Engage your brain's cognitive flexibility to find creative solutions.

The scientific foundations supporting the relationship between adversity and exemplary success are grounded in the brain's capacity for adaptation, growth, and evolution. Adversity cultivates resilience, triggers neuroplasticity, enhances problem-solving abilities, and fosters emotional regulation. By understanding these dynamics and applying common themes such as adopting a growth mindset, building resilience, embracing change, practicing emotional regulation, and fostering innovation, individuals can navigate adversity as a path not just to survival, but to thriving. The transformative power of adversity lies not solely in overcoming it but in leveraging it as a springboard toward a life brimming with fulfilment and success.

"Vipatteh parikalpyante mahatvaya cha sambhramah,
Adhiyante sarve yatra samare dheeratam gatah."

Translation:

"Adversity's trials sculpt the mighty, stoking determination's fire,

In the battlefield of challenges, the brave attain their truest desire."

As we journey through these narratives and delve into the science behind them, remember that adversity is not an obstacle but a catalyst. It is the crucible where grit and grace, determination, and adaptability, come together to forge not just success, but a life imbued with meaning and purpose.

> *"Look for the good in every situation, seek the valuable lesson in every setback, look for the solution to every problem. Think and talk continually about your goals." – Brian Tracy*

X

“Self-compassion & Self-Care”

Lasting Mental Well-Being

In the grand tale of our lives, we often find intricate patterns of ambitions and dreams. We chase our goals with unwavering determination, guided by our ambitions and aspirations. Amidst this frenetic pursuit, we sometimes forget the vital thread that binds it all together - our mental and emotional well-being. Our mental health, much like our physical health, deserves diligent care and attention. In this relentless journey of professionals, where Grit and grace are their guiding stars, the concepts of self-compassion and self-care stand as pillars of strength.

Understanding Self-Compassion: Your Inner Friend

Picture this: You have a friend who is your unwavering pillar of support. This friend is there through thick and thin, offering a shoulder to lean on during tough times.

They listen without judgment, and their kindness knows no bounds. This friend, my dear readers, is none other than your inner voice of self-compassion. It's a voice that never berates you for your mistakes but rather extends a hand of understanding and warmth. This inner friend encourages you to treat yourself with the same kindness you'd bestow upon others. It's about recognizing your struggles without the weight of self-criticism and embracing your imperfections with open arms, all the while exuding Grit and grace. Cultivating self-compassion is akin to tending a garden. You start by acknowledging your feelings and experiences without judgment. Instead of saying, "I shouldn't feel this way," you utter, "It's okay to feel this way." This subtle shift in perspective allows you to validate your emotions, acknowledging their presence without harsh self-judgment.

Next, it's time to practice self-kindness. Picture a scenario where you've had a particularly challenging day at work. Instead of chastising yourself for every mistake, imagine saying, "It's alright, everyone has tough days." This self-kindness transforms your inner dialogue and has a profound impact on your emotional well-being. It's a testament to your Grit and grace.

Lastly, remember the principle of common humanity. It's the understanding that you're not alone in your struggles. Just as everyone encounters challenges in life, you are an integral part of this shared human experience. This realization breaks down the walls of isolation, fostering a sense of connection and empathy, nurturing your Grit and grace even in the face of adversity.

The Science Behind Self-Compassion: A Robust Foundation

Now, you might wonder, does this touchy-feely concept of self-compassion hold any water in the real world? Well, my fellow Grit & Grace enthusiasts, the answer is a resounding yes, backed by science. Numerous studies have linked self-compassion to a plethora of mental health benefits. It's like discovering the hidden gem of well-being. Research suggests that individuals who practice self-compassion experience lower levels of anxiety, depression, and stress. A notable study by Neff and Germer in 2013 revealed that self-compassion was intricately tied to greater emotional well-being and life satisfaction. These self-compassionate souls tend to have healthier self-esteem and overall psychological functioning. But it doesn't stop there. Self-compassion also plays a pivotal role in enhancing emotional intelligence – the capacity to understand and manage not only your emotions but also the emotions of others. When you treat yourself with compassion, you become more attuned to your emotions and can respond to them more healthily. This heightened emotional intelligence, in turn, improves your interactions with others, making you a paragon of Grit and grace.

Self-Care: Nourishing Your Soul

Now that we've delved into the depths of self-compassion, it's time to explore its partner in well-being: self-care. Picture self-care as the oxygen mask on an aero plane. In those critical moments, you're advised to secure your mask before assisting others. Similarly, taking care of yourself is not selfish; it's essential for your well-being and your ability to care for others. Self-care involves indulging in activities that recharge your energy and bring you joy. It can be as simple as taking a leisurely walk in the park, getting lost in the pages of an engaging book, or spending quality time with your loved ones. It also encompasses maintaining a healthy lifestyle by prioritizing adequate sleep, nourishing your body with wholesome food, and staying physically active.

Managing Anxiety: The Calm Amidst the Storm

In the tumultuous sea of life, anxiety can sometimes swell like a storm, threatening to capsize our resolve. It's in these moments that the principles of self-compassion and self-care can offer solace and resilience. One powerful technique to manage anxiety is the art of deep breathing. Think of it as inflating a balloon. Take a slow, deliberate breath in through your nose, allowing your abdomen to rise like a balloon filling with air. Then, exhale gently through your mouth, visualizing the tension and worry leaving your body with each breath. This simple yet potent practice triggers your body's relaxation response, calming the turbulent waters of your mind. It's a practice that embodies both Grit and grace, a harmonious dance between determination and serenity.

Cultivating Resilience: The Essence of Inner Strength

Resilience is the fortress within you that withstands life's tempests. Imagine it as a rubber ball - when life throws it to the ground, it bounces back with unwavering strength. To cultivate resilience, focus on your strengths. Reflect on the challenges you've triumphed over in the past and how they've shaped you. This introspection serves as a potent reminder of your ability to adapt, evolve, and emerge stronger from adversity. It's a testament to your Grit and grace, for it is through these trials that your character is forged.

Promoting Emotional Intelligence

Emotional intelligence, my dear readers, is the bridge that connects you to the hearts and minds of others. To strengthen this bridge, practice the art of active listening.

When someone speaks, give them your full attention, tuning in not only to their words but also to the emotions underlying them. Respond with empathy and understanding, forging a deeper connection that transcends mere words. This bridge-building exercise enhances your emotional intelligence, allowing you to navigate the complex landscape of human emotions with finesse Grit and grace.

The Modern Relevance of Self-Compassion: A Post-Pandemic Perspective

As we stand on the cusp of a new era, the world has irrevocably changed. The pandemic hurled us into a maelstrom of unprecedented challenges, from isolation-induced loneliness to the constant barrage of uncertainty. In this context, self-compassion has emerged as an anchor, a lifeline that keeps us tethered to our well-being. The post-pandemic world demands resilience and adaptability - qualities that find fertile ground in the garden of self-compassion. As we navigate the aftermath of the pandemic, being kind to ourselves is not just a nicety; it's a necessity. Self-compassion equips us to cope with the lingering echoes of stress and anxiety. It whispers to us in our moments of doubt, reminding us of the Grit and grace that carried us through the storm. In a world where the relentless pursuit of perfection and ceaseless comparison often dominate our thoughts, self-compassion serves as a powerful antidote. It encourages us to embrace our humanness, imperfections, and all. By doing so, we fortify the foundations of our mental and emotional well-being, standing firm with unwavering Grit and grace.

Conclusion: Paving the Way to Lasting Well-Being

In the grand mosaic of life, just as a well-tended garden yields vibrant and beautiful flowers, nurturing our self-compassion and practicing self-care can lead to a flourishing mental and emotional landscape. Through simple acts of kindness to ourselves, we can navigate the labyrinthine challenges of life with greater resilience, foster emotional intelligence that bridges connections with others, and cultivate a sense of Grit and grace that defines our character. The scientific evidence supporting the transformative effects of self-compassion on our mental health is resounding. It underscores the significance of self-compassion in the modern world, particularly in the wake of the pandemic. As we journey through the vicissitudes of life, let us not forget to treat ourselves with the same compassion and care we so readily offer to others. In doing so, we pave the way for a brighter, more emotionally resilient future. It's a future where Grit and grace intertwine, guiding us through the ebb and flow of life's magnificent tapestry, and nurturing our mental and emotional well-being as we dare to dream and strive for greatness.

here are key takeaways from the chapter on "The Power of Self-Compassion and Self-Care for Mental Well-Being":

- Self-Compassion is Your Inner Friend: Think of self-compassion as having a supportive friend within you. This friend is always kind, understanding, and non-judgmental. Treat yourself with the same kindness and understanding you would offer to a friend in times of need. Grit and grace aren't just about determination; they're also about being gentle with yourself.
- Cultivate Self-Compassion Like a Garden: Developing self-compassion is like tending to a garden. Start by acknowledging your feelings without judgment. Practice self-kindness by treating yourself with

gentleness during difficult times. Remember that you are part of a shared human experience, which can help you feel more connected and less isolated.

- Science Supports Self-Compassion: Scientific research shows that self-compassion is linked to improved mental health. It can reduce anxiety, depression, and stress while enhancing emotional well-being and life satisfaction. Self-compassion also fosters emotional intelligence, improving your relationships with others.
- Managing Anxiety with Self-Compassion: When anxiety feels overwhelming, practice deep breathing to trigger your body's relaxation response. It's a technique that combines determination (Grit) with serenity (Grace) to calm your mind during stressful moments.
- Resilience and Emotional Intelligence: Cultivating resilience involves reflecting on past challenges and understanding how they've made you stronger. Strengthen emotional intelligence by actively listening to others and responding empathetically. These qualities embody both Grit and grace, fostering better relationships and personal growth.

Remember, the journey to well-being is a blend of self-compassion and self-care, a path where Grit and grace walk hand in hand, guiding you towards a brighter, emotionally resilient future.

> " *"Rest and self-care are so important. When you take time to replenish your spirit, it allows you to serve others from the overflow. You cannot serve from an empty vessel."*
> *— Eleanor Brownn* "

STRATEGIES FOR TAMING THE TOUGH TIMES"

Throughout this captivating journey, we've delved deep into the heart of resilience, uncovering its profound significance, tracing its roots in scientific research, and weaving its magnificent tapestry through real-life stories that inspire and uplift. Now, as we stand at the culmination of this transformative odyssey, we find ourselves armed not only with knowledge but also with a profound sense of purpose. It's time to embark on a voyage of self-discovery, where we shall build resilience, embrace the winds of change, and flourish amidst the tempests of adversity.

Embrace the Power of Mindset

As we embark on this journey, imagine the mighty Dwayne "The Rock" Johnson, a living testament to grit and grace. Consider the setbacks he faced, the mountains he climbed, and how each challenge transformed him into an even stronger force. What's his secret? It's the power of a growth mindset. A growth mindset sees challenges as opportunities for growth, not insurmountable barriers. When life hurls obstacles in your path, ask yourself, "What can I learn from this?" This subtle shift in perspective can change the course of your life. Challenges, when seen through the lens of a growth mindset, become stepping stones on your path to resilience, not stumbling blocks.

Nurture Self-Compassion

Now, envision yourself as your own best friend. How would you treat yourself when the storms of life rage on? Would you chastise yourself or offer a comforting embrace? Take a cue from the great Oprah Winfrey, an icon of resilience who advocates treating oneself with the same kindness bestowed upon cherished friends. In moments of failure or stumbles, adopt Oprah's approach. Be gentle with yourself, and acknowledge your humanity without judgment. This practice is the heartbeat of resilience, nurturing your self-worth. It's like a warm, reassuring hug from your soul, reminding you of your strength and your capacity for grit and grace.

Embrace Change as a Constant

Change, my dear readers, is the river that flows through the landscape of life, ceaselessly and inevitably. It is the only constant we can truly rely on. So why fear it? Instead, let's learn to embrace change as an opportunity for growth, much like a graceful dancer twirling in the spotlight. Pause for a moment and reflect on the changes you've navigated successfully in the past. Think about how each of those experiences made you stronger, wiser, and more resilient. This shift in perspective empowers you to approach new challenges with unwavering confidence, just as the indomitable Sir Richard Branson did when he transformed from a modest record store owner into a global mogul through the sheer power of grit and grace.

Develop Problem-Solving Skills

Resilience isn't just about bouncing back; it's about finding ingenious solutions to life's labyrinthine problems. It's about breaking down these problems into manageable fragments, much like an artist sculpting a masterpiece from a block of marble. Seek wisdom from mentors or friends who have traversed similar treacherous paths. Consider the extraordinary Malala Yousafzai, a beacon of resilience who stood tall for education in the face of adversity. She transformed her ordeal into a global mission. Embrace Malala's problem-solving spirit. Break your difficulties into bite-sized pieces and seek guidance from your mentors—the Yodas of your life. This strategic approach will not only sharpen your problem-solving skills but will also fortify your arsenal of grit and grace.

Practice Self-Care Rituals

Imagine Hugh Jackman, the versatile actor, and his unwavering commitment to self-care. He extols the virtues of daily rituals like meditation and exercise. Just as Jackman carves out time for self-care, curate a routine filled with activities that rejuvenate your spirit, whether it's an invigorating morning jog or a moment of mindful contemplation. These rituals bestow clarity and vitality, enabling you to confront life's challenges with renewed vigor, imbued with the essence of grit and grace. It's akin to tending to a precious garden within you, ensuring it thrives even in the harshest of seasons.

Foster a Supportive Network

In the world of music, imagine Taylor Swift, navigating the tumultuous sea of stardom with grace and resilience. Through the highs and lows, she had a robust support network of fellow artists and devoted fans. You too can cultivate such a circle of confidants. Surround yourself with friends, family, and mentors who uplift and guide you. Share your stories, your struggles, and your triumphs with them. This network doesn't just provide emotional support; it reinforces your resilience by reminding you that you're never alone on this magnificent journey of grit and grace.

Cultivate Adaptability

Picture Elon Musk, a modern-day visionary, navigating uncharted territories, from electric vehicles to space exploration. He embodies adaptability, a cornerstone of resilience. Challenge yourself to step out of your comfort zone, to embrace new experiences. As you navigate unfamiliar terrain, you'll develop the flexibility needed to navigate unexpected changes with grace. Just as Musk pivots his ventures with ease, venturing into the unknown cultivates the adaptability that grit and grace demand, enabling you to ride the waves of change with elegance and fortitude.

Practice Gratitude

Now, let's delve into the practice of gratitude. Imagine radiating positivity through our daily gratitude practice. Even amidst life's storms, we find reasons to be thankful. Each day, pause to reflect on three things you're grateful for, no matter how seemingly insignificant they may be. Gratitude fosters a positive mindset, guiding your focus towards the facets of your life that are thriving, even amidst challenges. It's like a beacon of light that pierces through the darkest clouds, reminding you of the beauty that exists in every corner of life. Gratitude is the heartbeat of grit and grace.

Embody Emotional Regulation

Think of the leader of the largest democracy on the face of the earth during the pandemic Narendra Modi; the embodiment of poise in the face of adversity. He understands the power of emotional regulation. It's about practicing mindfulness and becoming aware of your emotions without judgment. When life hurls its storms your way, take a deep breath, pause, and regulate your emotions before responding. This skill empowers you to approach challenges with the clarity and composure of a seasoned captain steering a ship through turbulent waters.

Set Realistic Goals

Visualize Virat Kohli, a symbol of setting and achieving goals with unwavering focus. He breaks down his long-term ambitions into achievable milestones. Every step forward, no matter how small, fuels his journey of grit and grace. You too can adopt this approach. Divide your grand dreams into manageable steps. Celebrate your progress along the way, regardless of how modest it may seem. This methodology prevents feelings of being overwhelmed and provides a sense of accomplishment that fuels your ongoing journey of grit and grace.

Transforming Your Resilience: The Symphony of Grit & Grace

As we stand on the precipice of our resilience journey, let us harness the collective wisdom of these extraordinary trailblazers. The path before us, illuminated by science and narrated through the lives of luminaries, is a testament to the extraordinary strength within us all.

Just as these luminaries conquered adversity, so too can we. Equipped with these actionable strategies, let us dare to construct our resilience blueprint. Let's turn challenges into triumphs, navigate the ever-changing tides of life with grace, and ultimately thrive amidst the grand tapestry of existence. your resilience journey is a tribute to your inner power, waiting to be transformed into a magnificent symphony of grit and grace. So, my fellow travellers, let's set forth on this exhilarating adventure together, knowing that we possess the tools, the knowledge, and the spirit to conquer whatever storms may come our way. In the end, it's not just about resilience; it's about embodying the essence of grit and grace in every step we take.

> “*"Resilience comes when we accept what is unchangeable, but don't accept that everything is unchangeable" - Lord Sri Krishna*”

www.ingramcontent.com/pod-product-compliance
Lightning Source LLC
LaVergne TN
LVHW091118150826
845673LV00002B/888

* 9 7 9 8 8 9 1 3 3 1 1 6 7 *